SIMPLE SELF-CARE FOR THERAPISTS

A NORTON PROFESSIONAL BOOK

SIMPLE SELF-CARE FOR THERAPISTS

RESTORATIVE PRACTICES TO WEAVE THROUGH YOUR WORKDAY

ASHLEY DAVIS BUSH

W. W NORTON & COMPANY
NEW YORK | LONDON

Printed in the United States of America
First Edition

For information about permission to reproduce selections from this book, write to Permissions, W. W. Norton & Company, Inc., 500 Fifth Avenue, New York, NY 10110

For information about special discounts for bulk purchases, please contact W. W. Norton
Special Sales at specialsales@wwnorton.com or 800–233–4830

Manufacturing by Maple Press
Production manager: Chris Critelli

Library of Congress Cataloging-in-Publication Data

Bush, Ashley Davis.
Simple self-care for therapists : restorative practices to weave through your workday / Ashley Davis Bush.—First edition.
pages cm.—(A Norton professional book)
Includes bibliographical references and index.
ISBN 978–0-393–70837–0 (hardcover)
1. Psychotherapists—Job stress. 2. Psychotherapists—Mental health.
3. Burn out (Psychology)—Prevention. I. Title.
RC451.4.P79B876 2015
616.89'14092—dc23
2014044265

ISBN: 978–0-393–70837–0

W. W. Norton & Company, Inc., 500 Fifth Avenue, New York, N.Y. 10110
www.wwnorton.com
W. W. Norton & Company Ltd., Castle House, 75/76 Wells Street, London W1T 3QT

1 2 3 4 5 6 7 8 9 0

To my North Star

Contents

PART III THE RESOURCES

Acknowledgments

FIRST AND FOREMOST, I extend my deepest gratitude to Andrea Costella Dawson at W.W. Norton. I can say that this book literally would not be in the world if it had not been for her vision and initial enthusiasm. I thank the entire W.W.Norton team, including Ben Yarling and Kathryn Moyer, for their skill in bringing this book to life.

I am also delighted to thank my amazing literary agent, John Willig. I am indeed fortunate to have such a skilled veteran in the publishing industry in my corner. John is a pro and an all round great guy.

I have been fortunate to chat either in person or on the phone with many superb therapists who shared their ideas, challenges, practices, and struggles with me. Thank you, thank you, thank you.

I thank my colleagues who keep me on track personally and professionally: Nancy Webb, Candace Wheeler, Sue Mautz, Claire Houston, Lesley Zarat, and Denise Lamothe.

As for my family, I am deeply honored to have been supported and loved by my mother, Peyton Lewis and my father, William P. Davis for over 50 years now. I thank my five children, who I hope will spend their lives perfecting the art of self-care: Elizabeth, Channing, Setse, Victoria, and Inle.

And, saving the best for last, I thank my adored and cherished husband Daniel. Daniel is my collaborator, first editor, colleague, best friend, soul mate, true love, and rock. Daniel not only cares for me but also encourages my own self-care. He helps me to be my best self and do my best work in the world.

SIMPLE SELF-CARE FOR THERAPISTS

Introduction

I DON'T actually enjoy going to the dentist, but I certainly do enjoy the feeling of freshly cleaned teeth. And I'm fond of my dental hygienist. She is always upbeat, positive, and full of enthusiasm for life and for dental hygiene.

She knows that I am a writer and is consistently curious about my latest project. She has followed biyearly updates of my books in their various phases of development, from the proposal to the writing and the production to the promotion.

One bright spring afternoon, as I sat in the chair preparing myself for discomfort, she asked, "So what book are you working on now?"

Quickly, before the stainless steel tool entered my mouth, I answered, "I'm writing a book about self-care for therapists."

She considered this for a moment, inserted the mirror on a metal stick, and quipped, "Do therapists actually need self-care?"

I practically choked on the mirror, at which point she clarified, "What I mean is, do they need more self-care than other workers and professionals?"

True, all humans, regardless of their jobs, simply need self-care. Teachers and bank managers, waitresses and receptionists, attorneys and pilots, accountants and dental hygienists all suffer job stresses, experience fatigue, are susceptible to burnout, and *need* self-care to remain healthy. Everybody suffers less and is more available when they take care of themselves. This is especially true for the psychotherapist.

For therapists, intentional self-care is a survival tool. Why? Because in sitting with and treating the suffering of others every day, we are exposed to pain and trauma and the inevitable effects it has on our nervous systems and bodies. We are containers for story after story of unhappiness and human struggle, with a never-ending responsibility to hold the tragic secrets of others. If we don't take care of ourselves, we can't do our work effectively.

In her book *Trauma Stewardship*, Laura van Dernoot Lipsky points out that exposure to trauma is part and parcel for those working in the helping professions. Trauma exposure changes us, sometimes in ways that are draining, challenging, and traumatizing. Intentional self-care practices are not only essential to successfully navigating those changes but are also our methods for stress prevention, the tools that help us titrate our exposure to stress and trauma without internalizing it.

I have a friend who says that working in this field is like inhaling second hand smoke all day long. Day after day, we insert ourselves intimately into the lives of people who are broken and hurting. We breathe the smoke of harrowing stories of abuse, addiction, loss, conflict, and misery even as we witness incredible feats of survival and resilience. We're impacted profoundly by what we take in whether we realize it or not. The practice of self-care is like an invisible oxygen mask that allows us to sit, listen, and help day after day despite the smoke. Wearing this mask puts us in the best position to offer oxygen to our clients when they are ready.

THE INSTRUMENT

Helpers and healers of all types—psychotherapists, social workers, mental health counselors, life coaches, marriage and family therapists, pastoral counselors, psychologists, psychiatrists, psychiatric nurses, human service workers—are in a unique position on the front lines of humanity. Unlike the person on the street who sees only the faces and outfits of those who pass by, we as helpers see behind the masks of polite society. We become privy to the whole person—the feelings, thoughts, and life story behind the jewelry and ties.

We become witnesses to people's lives, and are sometimes the only person who truly hears their stories. And we do this by showing up, being present, listening, opening our hearts, and connecting, one soul to another. We know that the strength of successful therapy hinges on the relationship between therapist and client. It is less relevant whether you practice CBT, DBT, or EFT. The client doesn't care whether you're a Freudian, a Jungian, or a Russian. In spite of your interpretations and interventions, clients respond to your presence and your essence.

Being a therapist is a bit like being a singer—the instrument is ourselves. We are responsible for the sound, the tenor, the timbre, the vibrato, and the tone. And because of that, we need to keep our instrument, *our presence*, well cared for.

As helpers, caring for our instrument becomes something

of a serious ethical issue. When we don't keep ourselves 'well tuned,' not only is our ability to help others compromised but, when our stuff becomes their stuff, we cause harm to our clients. Picture a therapist whose uncared for self is stressed, burdened, and overwhelmed, whose clients' trauma has become his own, whose long hours and repeated frustrations have engendered apathy and cynicism. Picture the therapist who brings that troubled mind, those distressing emotions, and that stressed body into session with a client. Rather than helping his client, that therapist's contagious negative energy actually infects his client. It's our ethical obligation, both to us and our clients, to keep ourselves as instruments in top condition.

OK. Maybe I've convinced you or maybe you were already convinced that self-care is essential to good clinical practice. But the elephant in every therapist's room is the question, "Where is the time for self-care?" Will self-care become one more item on your endless to-do list? Will self-care become a burden, a necessary chore that you're bound to fail at because you don't have enough time, energy, or money to do one more single thing, even a really good thing?

PARADIGM SHIFT

I'd like to offer you the distinction between macro-self-care and micro-self-care. Macro-self-care is the important traditional category of self-care that includes the big stuff: vacations, exercise, social interactions, hobbies, supervision, adequate sleep, a healthy diet, and massages. These activities can be valuable, even essential self-care practices but they all require some larger combination of time, effort, and financial resources.

Micro-self-care, on the other hand, refers to practices that are simple enough to fit into your existing schedule, your current energy level, and your budget. Micro-practices are based on the concept that self-care is possible one bite-sized piece at a time. Calm, awareness, rejuvenation, and balance can be summoned in the moments between and during normal activities. Micro-self-care is about coming home to yourself intentionally during any part of your everyday activities.

The practices that I introduce in this book will open up a world of daily micro-self-care possibilities. They are small but effective, designed with limited time and energy in mind. More importantly, each practice is simple and practical enough to become a habit in your life, rewiring your brain toward awareness, serenity, and well-being. You don't have to wait until retirement, vacation, spa day, or the empty nest to take care of yourself. Nor will you have to wait until you get home from work, or until the weekend arrives. The tools described in the following pages are designed for you to weave through your workday. Now you can embrace the lifelong journey of self-care outside and inside the office.

This idea of intentionally developing micro-self-care practices has never been more important. In a world that relies on constant stimulation, 24/7 accessibility, and multitasking, we hardly know how or when to hit the pause button. Micro-self-care practices bring self-awareness, self-compassion, and self-healing into the trenches of our busy days and allow us to be more effective healers. Regular micro-self-care can make the difference between being the stressed out data junkie and the wise Zen apprentice, the difference between vicarious trauma and groundedness.

This book is about learning to hit the pause button and developing an interior landscape that is resistant to the minefields of our work. Dipping into the well of your own internal resources will revive and refresh you in unexpected ways. The result of learning some of these practices is that you will be more emotionally vibrant, present, attuned, and available to all those around you.

SELF-CARE 101

I have never understood why graduate programs in the human services don't require a course on the basics of self-care. Given the high levels of trauma exposure that counselors encounter and the high frequency with which they work alone, it seems only logical they learn skills to stay healthy, safe, and productive.

In their book, *Leaving it at the Office*, John Norcross and James Guy, two of the foremost clinical researchers of therapist self-care write: "Self-care is not a narcissistic luxury to be filled as time permits; it is a human requisite, a clinical necessity, and an ethical imperative" (p. 14). I agree. Clinicians who don't take care of themselves face stress, burnout, and the negative mental, physical, and emotional responses to trauma exposure. Clients will always be helped more by therapists who are aware, healthy, and centered.

But alas, they didn't require a self-care course twenty-five years ago when I was in social work school nor did they require this course one year ago when my husband finished his degree in mental health counseling. So consider this book your crash course in the basics of self-care—a primer in the core skills and daily habits that will make you a happier, emotionally sound, and effective professional.

FULL OR EMPTY?

I recently gave a professional presentation titled, *The Critical Importance of Self-Care*. Imagine, for a moment, that you're in the audience:

As you watch, I hold up an empty teacup and say, "This cup represents a therapist who doesn't take good care of herself. You can see here that the cup is empty and stained, here a hairline fracture, and there, a slight chip. This therapist is suffering from burnout, vicarious trauma, and compassion fatigue. This therapist is exhausted, stressed, and depleted. She is running on empty."

Now watch as I hold in one hand a different, clean teacup and, in the other hand, several wrapped chocolate truffles. "This therapist," I say, "is prioritizing self-care—both macro and micro. She exercises, sleeps well, and develops her hobbies." I drop one and then another chocolate into the cup. "This therapist," I continue, "learns ways to ground herself (a third chocolate), energize (a fourth), and relax (a fifth), during her regular workdays. She takes care of herself outside the office and brings self-care practices into the office."

This second teacup is now stuffed with chocolate truffles. Watch as I set the two cups side by side—one empty and the other overflowing.

"Which therapist would you rather work with?" I ask.

Pause.

"Which therapist would you rather be?"

THE STRUCTURE OF THE BOOK

This book will help you become the therapist who is an overflowing teacup, so to speak, with abundant resources for yourself and to share.

Part I of this book includes several chapters that set the stage for understanding both the complexities of self-care and the dangers of skimping on self-care. Chapter 1 takes a look at the macro spectrum of traditional practices from healthcare to balance to indulgences. Chapter 2 looks at the psychological resistances that often get in the way of making self-care a priority or reality. Chapter 3 describes the three main dangers lurking in our profession: burnout, compassion fatigue, and vicarious trauma. Understanding these risks clarifies the urgent need—indeed the ethical imperative—for making self-care habitual.

Part II offers a sample day for micro-self-care a paradigm that repositions self-care from an after-hours indulgence to a during-hours workday necessity. I present ten micro-self-care practices that can easily be woven into your workday.

Finally, Part III offers "The Resources," sixty additional restorative practices to weave throughout your workdays. These are organized into three categories: practices for grounding, energizing, and relaxing. Each are vital areas of focus because they offer antidotes to the three common pathologies suffered by therapists and other helpers: vicarious trauma, compassion fatigue, and burnout.

Although I illustrate many of the practices with stories from my own experience in private practice, the micro-self-care strategies in this book are applicable to a wide variety of professional settings. Because therapists engage in a diverse array of professional duties, many of which take place out of the private therapy room, these practices are also easily integrated into home visits, group therapy situations, staff meetings, workshops, lecturing, writing, supervising, and supervision.

Your goal should be to choose micro-self-care practices that work best for your individual situation and needs. To that end, I have attempted to structure the presentation of practices in a way that makes them easy to quickly scan. Each of the self-care practices is presented in four parts: *what* (a description of the practice), *when* (a suggested prompt), *why* (a description of the purpose), and a clinical or personal anecdote (a real life illustration of its use and value). All of the practices conclude with a reflection question to take your experience deeper.

A note regarding prompts: Whether you use the given prompt or come up with your own, it is important to remember that prompts are essential components of good habits. Every good habit is wired into your brain with a trigger. The trigger is some circumstance or feeling that prompts, or initiates, your habit. When you reach for your orange juice in the morning, your vitamin habit is 'prompted'. Likewise, you can train your brain to practice gratitude every time you reach for the doorknob. Prompts are crucial for a good practice to evolve into a healthy habit.

Unless otherwise noted, the clinical examples are composites with heavily changed identifying details to protect privacy. Any dialogue or story that you recognize is purely coincidental.

You will find that not all of the practices resonate with your own personal preferences. I suggest that you take what works for you and leave the rest. Maybe you'll discover that a few of them become foundational daily practices while others you use on occasion. As time goes by, many will even begin to fill your toolbox of self-soothing techniques that you share with clients.

Because we also crave novelty, you may find that you use some tools now and later switch to others . Use the book in the way that most makes sense to you. There is no right or wrong. Each practice is a portal into a healthier world of being with yourself and in your profession. Using even one of them repetitively will begin to carve new neural pathways of well-being in your brain.

If you are a student or new to the profession, you may find it instructive to read this book cover to cover. I present an array of clinical anecdotes and illustrative vignettes that offer a range of circumstances you may encounter as you move forward in your career. Although your clients and the circumstances of your work will be unique, reading into the experiences of seasoned counselors (*On Being a Therapist* by Jeffrey Kottler and *The Making of a Therapist* by Louis Cozolino come to mind) is a good way to get the lay of the land as you prepare your initial toolbox of self-care practices.

For my experienced colleagues, I've tried to organize this volume as a go-to resource book. Each self-care practice works independently. You may find it helpful to scan the practices at first and notice which you're drawn to. You may be more attracted to visualization tools and mindfulness practices, or you may find that the tools based in somatic empathy and body physiology are a better fit with your perspective and work situation.

So read on to learn about simple daily habits for self-care at home and at the office, on weekdays and weekends. Whether it's your first day of work or you're on the verge of retirement, may you enjoy each day left of your career and may each of those days—and all days—be filled with gentle self-care practices.

PART I

THE FOUNDATION

CHAPTER 1

ESSENTIALS OF SELF-CARE

A GUEST on my online talk radio program, *Embracing Change*, was telling me about her "Word of the Year" program. A life coach, she was describing a practice in which she selects a single word to be her guiding compass for the year.

This spin on the New Year's resolution was sure to be far easier and more effective than a hokey January promise, long forgotten by February. "When your word finds you," she proclaims, "you spend the year living into it, absorbing it, and watching it transform your life."

"So give me an example," I prompted, "of how a word can reshape your life. What was your word last year?"

"Self-care," she proclaimed.

Amazing, I thought. Self-care, of course, had been my mantra as I researched, developed, and wrote this book. I was curious how self-care had changed her. "What did you discover about your life?" I probed.

With authentic enthusiasm she answered, "I always thought I was kind of good at self-care, but I realized last year that I really needed to take it up a notch. I began to make it a priority, to schedule it and make it happen. Now, it's completely second nature."

"And has this shift improved your life?"

"Not only has it improved my life," she gushed, "but it has improved my husband's life, my kids' lives, and my clients' lives. When I was depleted, I was no good to anyone, really. When I intentionally took care of myself, I had tons more to share."

Perfect. She was a walking advertisement for what I was preaching. When you feel better, the people around you also feel better. Everybody wins.

SO WHAT IS SELF-CARE ANYWAY?

What comes to mind when you think of *self-care*? Do you imagine a hot bath, good book, or morsel of imported chocolate? Do you see a fishing pole, beach, or forest trail? Do you conjure the image of a couch in front of a television, massage table, or a seat at the fifty-yard line? Do you envision vitamins, a treadmill, a meditation cushion, or dental floss?

Obviously, the idea of self-care is multi-layered and highly individual. What might be heaven for you (cooking a gourmet dinner) could easily be my hell. And while I might love doing jigsaw puzzles, they give you a headache. There are those who swear by gratitude practices and those who wouldn't go a day without a quiet walk. Still, I think we can agree that there are certain common denominators in the art of self-care.

At the core, self-care practices are the activities that make and keep us healthy and happy. They may be preventative, protective, or curative. They all involve nurturing the self and at their best are the seeds for growing self-compassion. To unpack the idea of self-care, I'd like to clarify the difference again between macro- and micro-self-care that I described in the Introduction. Macro-self-care is the traditional stuff that we do for rest, relaxation, entertainment, fitness, and rejuvenation. These big activities, as you know, also take larger chunks of time and resources. And sometimes they might feel separate from, rather than integrated into, our daily lives.

Micro-self-care practices, the simple daily tasks that we can do to nurture, protect, and heal ourselves during our regular days, have the integrative capacity to improve our mood, decrease our emotional reactivity, and increase our mind-body awareness. Still, macro-self-care is an important component of the therapist's self-care protocol. Therefore, before we examine micro-self-care practices, the primary focus of this book, I'd like to invite you to reflect briefly with me on the role of larger scale self-care practices in your life. I categorize the three primary dimensions of macro-self-care as healthcare, balance, and treats.

SELF-CARE AS HEALTH CARE

I've heard it said that 'health is wealth.' And it's true that when we feel physically healthy, everything seems easier. Alternately, when we feel physically compromised, life is a struggle. Shawn Talbot, a nutritional biochemist, uses the term 'vigor' to refer to the sustained mood state of physical, emotional and mental maximum energy (2011). He points out that vigor is best maintained with sufficient sleep, effective exercise, and healthy nutrition. Using his template, I'm going to skim the surface of the basics for consideration.

Sleep

Being an avid nine-hour a night sleeper, sleep deprivation for me is essentially torture. As therapists, our wide-eyed attention and clarity of awareness is essential to the work we do with our clients. You wouldn't intentionally show up for your clients drunk or in a similarly compromised state. Sleep deprivation stresses our ability to think clearly, stay present and, literally, stay awake. According to the "2009 Sleep in America Poll" conducted by the National Sleep Foundation, people who report too little sleep also report being less able to perform daytime basics such as efficient work, exercise, healthy eating, sex, and leisure activities.

I urge you to reflect seriously on how the following key lifestyle factors affect your sleep and ultimately your ability to be fully with your clients (adapted from The National Sleep Foundation, 2014):

- Your sleeping environment impacts the quality of your sleep. Is your bedroom pleasant, dark enough, quiet enough?
- Napping affects your ability to sleep at night. Are you napping over thirty minutes during the day and having difficulty sleeping at night?

- Your bed should only be used for sleep or sex. Do you work, play, or watch TV from your bed?
- A regular bedtime schedule is a way to train your body to fall asleep when it is time. Do you vary your bedtime routine?
- Stimulants and depressants like caffeine, nicotine, and alcohol can disrupt your ability to fall asleep and stay asleep. What are the effects of your drinking or smoking habits on the quality of your sleep?
- Exercise late in the day can keep you awake. Is your exercise schedule affecting your sleep?

Exercise

Unless you've been living in a cave for the past three decades, you know that exercise is one of the cornerstones of good health. If nothing else, exercise may be the best cure for stress, depression, insomnia, low energy levels, and depressed immune response. In the long run, exercise slows the body's aging process, and reduces the risk of cancer and other diseases. Becoming physically fit can be as easy as a brisk thirty-minute walk three times a week. Fitness creates an environment for effective micro-self-care practices—the trick is finding something you enjoy doing so you'll stick with it.

Diet

We often forget that, except for the air we breathe, every cell, molecule, and chemical in our body comes from the food and beverages we ingest. Our body chemistry, especially that of our blood and brain, is changed and maintained hourly by the food we put in our mouths. Nutrients literally are the building blocks to good health. In other words, poor nutrition will jeopardize every other attempt to improve your wellness.

The topics of nutrition and healthy eating are well researched, yet much debated. It is not my intention to offer advice on the best diet for you. If you take what you eat seriously, then education and awareness are your best guides. How does your body respond to sugar? Have you ever selectively removed dairy, wheat, gluten, or other ingredients to see how you feel? Do you know what chemicals are in the foods that you eat? Have you ever had your blood tested for nutrient levels? Whether you're gluten free, dairy free, meat free or sugar free, your body will always be changing and so will the way that your body processes and metabolizes certain foods. The path towards your best nutrition starts with awareness of what you are eating and how it makes you feel.

SELF-CARE AS BALANCE

My colleague, Jill, and I were discussing the benefits of self-care on a late summer afternoon. "It's almost as if self-care isn't a big enough word," I said.

"You know," she replied, "we sit all day with the weight of our clients' torn and broken souls. We need to have equally weighty concern for ourselves. We need to offset the heavy load of our work. We need ballast."

The nautical term *ballast* refers to the heavy material in the hull of a ship (such as water, sand, or cargo) that creates stability. Without ballast, a ship is top heavy and could capsize. Similarly, without ballast in our lives, weighty self-nurturance to balance the heavy weight of our exposure to suffering, we too are likely to capsize.

The following components of living (relationships, hobbies, community, and spirituality) are the sort of cargo that we need to create ballast as we negotiate the tricky seas of psychotherapy. They keep us stable, balanced, on course, and afloat.

Relationships

As therapists, we know that most psychotherapy is all about relationships. Unhealthy relationships are the basis for most trauma and unhappiness that we see in our therapy rooms. Healthy relationships (including the one our client has with us) are the basis for growth and healing. We, like our clients, are relational beings and our wellbeing is at once a response to the health of our relationships and an indicator of our ability to form healthy relationships. Maintaining satisfying, mutual relationships outside the therapy room offers you the necessary perspective and connection that you need to maintain healthy therapeutic relationships with your clients.

All kinds of relationships, whether with an intimate partner, children, extended family, family of origin, dear friends, neighbors, or pets take time and energy. The investment pays off, however, because they create the balance necessary for a healthy therapeutic life.

Hobbies

Hobbies are the unique self in action. They are the essence of self-expression and creativity—the gift of fun and joy. Hobbies enrich your connection to your interests and ground you in a broader prospective. Whether it is knitting, gardening, journaling, coin collecting, motorcycling, singing, acting, ballroom dancing, playing an instrument, photography, or beach combing, listen to your inner self and balance your life with a hobby.

Community

Community involvement not only creates a context for developing and maintaining healthy relationships, it is also a source for emotional support and social variety. Further, it offers a venue for service. Community connections (be it with town, school, church, or specific interests) create a system of roots that ground your life.

Do you have a social group that allows you to leave your therapist hat at home? Find ways to connect with and contribute to your community and reflect on how you begin to feel as a result.

Spirituality

Whether you ignite your inner flame through prayer, meditation, nature, poetry, song, volunteerism, or some other practice, connecting to something greater than yourself has a weighty impact on your life. Spirituality for you may be very private and may even go by a different name. Or it may be very public and social. Under all its guises, spirituality has the fantastic ability to open our hearts, create perspective, and connect beyond ourselves.

In my work with grievers, I've noticed that those with a strong spiritual sense suffer less and transcend their loss more easily than individuals who grieve without a spiritual foundation. And of course, the basis for all twelve-step programs is about connecting with a higher power. Living a spiritual life has a healing quality to it.

As a therapist, if you open yourself to spirituality in your life, you invite the possibility of a faith that can fuel your sense of meaning in the world around you.

SO MUCH TO DO, SO LITTLE TIME

In order to make room for relationships, community, hobbies, and spirituality, you need to set limits in your professional life. Examples of such boundaries include: no clients on weekends; no more than five clients a day; no calls after 7 p.m.; no paperwork at home; no emails on Sundays; no more than forty hours a week of work; or no less than four weeks of vacation a year. Discover what is best and doable for you and then intentionally create a work setting and home environment that supports your limits.

Honor your natural rhythms by allowing a balance of productive versus leisure time. How much quiet time or leisure time you need will depend on your personality type and tendency toward introversion versus extroversion. Are you replenished by silence and solitude or by a night out with the guys? Know and respect your personality type and seek the kind of activities that fill and refresh you.

SELF-CARE AS TREATS

Like health care and balance, treats are key ingredients in the macro-self-care pie. Treats bring diversity, surprise, color, and celebration to our days. Treats ignite the fire of appreciation and playfulness. When we keep these fires burning, we feel good and subsequently do good work. Pepper your life with small rewards and simple pleasures that scream loudly "celebration!" (or whisper quietly, "yum").

Find the occasional and daily indulgences that create wonder just for you. If it's using the fine china and crystal, do it. If it's spending ten minutes playing a video game, do it. If it's a little beef jerky or a bon bon in the afternoon, have it. If you are partnered, sensual moments from kissing and caressing to joint bubble baths and full throttle sexual pleasure can be a treat.

Ultimately, treats are symbolic of an attitude of self-appreciation, even self-cherishing. According to your budget and your time constraints, build both regular and extra special treats into your days. This habit will create gems of joy in your life and help you feel valued.

Perhaps none of this is news to you. You already know that healthcare, balance, and treats are a recipe for great self-care. So why is it so hard to actually mix these crucial ingredients into our lives?

CHAPTER 2

THE CHALLENGES OF SELF-CARE

He leaned back in his creaky, old leather chair and adjusted his white clerical collar. "What would you say is your greatest weakness?" he asked quietly.

This wasn't a job interview or even a college admissions screening. I was being considered as an applicant for a prestigious private Episcopalian school in Dallas, Texas. I was in 7th grade.

I had just finished telling him about my greatest strength, that I was a hard worker . . . and very organized. (I thought I was clever to sneak in a second greatest strength.) But now, a weakness?

"Well, sir," I stammered, "I guess I'd have to say that . . . I'm selfish." I looked down, a bit ashamed.

He nodded thoughtfully. "Can you give me an example?" I shook my head "no," averting his gaze.

"Is this something that you've been told?" he probed gently.

I nodded my head "yes."

This thoughtful, silver-haired gentleman with crystal blue eyes leaned ever so slightly forward. "Self-care is often mistaken for selfishness," he whispered.

I had no idea what he meant.

"Taking care of yourself," he continued, "is one of the kindest things you can do for others. When your cup runneth over, you have more to share. Try to remember that."

As it turns out, I didn't end up going to that school but I did remember his advice. He was right. Self-care is often mistaken for selfishness.

IT'S BETTER TO . . .

Is there anyone who didn't grow up with this belief that it is better to give than to recieve? It's a cross-cultural rule of hospitality. It's in the *Bible*, for heaven's sake. We respect people who graciously give, who think of others before themselves. We admire individuals who are self-less, not selfish. In fact, people who take care of themselves before others are looked down upon, mistrusted and even sometimes judged as sinful.

Women, especially, are burdened by this mentality—particularly when they become mothers. I remember after my first baby was born, my mother-in-law at the time, a German WWII survivor, told me, "A mother's sacrificial love is the greatest gift. You must not think of yourself anymore." I honestly believe that dear Ingeborg, upon having oxygen masks on a plane fall from their storage berths, would absolutely not have put her mask on first. No way. No matter what the flight attendants told her.

Like Ingeborg, most of us, male or female, did not grow up in a family or culture that embraced self-care as an essential life skill. In fact, the term self-care may not even have been part of your vocabulary. The clients seem innumerable, mothers and fathers, bosses and employees, who have sat across from me, downtrodden from a lifetime of self sacrifice and overwork "for the sake of others." Suffering from anxiety, depression, panic attacks, burnout and exhaustion, they are victims of a culture that doesn't consider self-care essential to good health and human happiness. However, as a helper, not only is unmediated self-sacrifice harmful to you, it is harmful to your clients as your ability to function well is jeopardized. Self-care for the therapist is an ethical obligation.

CAREGIVER'S SYNDROME

"What are you writing about these days?" asked a dear colleague of mine, over lunch.

"I'm writing a book about self-care for therapists," I answered.

She shook her head, making a *tsk tsk* sound. She said slowly, "Therapists are *not* interested in self-care. In fact, they couldn't care less. They're only interested in helping other people."

I had to shake my head and make my own *tsk tsk*. "What they don't realize is that by taking care of themselves, they can be better at helping others. It's a win-win."

Unconvinced, my friend had the last word. "They'll still have a million excuses about why self-care won't work."

So I took it upon myself to conduct an informal survey, asking colleagues around the country about their self-care practices and whether they struggle with it or not.

Maybe my lunch friend was right because I heard a lot of excuses:

"I know self-care is a good idea, but I don't have enough time."
"I have a hard time saying *no* to people."
"Everything I like to do for self-care costs too much money!"
"I don't really need anything extra. I'm fine."
"I get filled up by helping others. I don't need more self-care than that."
"I already exercise and take vacations. That's enough."
"I have to connect with my clients' pain in order to help them. If I focus on myself, then I won't be able to focus on them."

Is self-care simply a luxury, available only to those with money and time? Is an iron will required to conjure up the desire and resolution to embrace self-care? Is it really that important? Why does self-care feel so inaccessible?

One thirty-something therapist specializing in marriage and family counseling offered me part of the answer. "I think it has something to do with guilt. We don't feel like we deserve to take care of ourselves." Bingo. Part of the answer for why we engage in chronic self-sacrifice is that we feel guilty for engaging in self-care. If self-care feels selfish to you, then you are not alone.

IT'S YOUR CHOICE

One of my self-care teachers, Alaya Chadwick, author of *Wake up to Your (W)hole Life* took the concept of self-care to a whole new level. "There are only two choices in life," she intoned, "self-care or self-violence. When you don't take care of yourself, you're being violent to yourself and to those around you." To this group of self-care pioneers who met over the course of six months as part of an "Ethics with a Heart" course, our fearless leader offered a very powerful template through which to view self-care.

At first, I thought, *Jeeez. That seems a bit extreme, don't you think? Violence, really?*

Over the course of those six months, Alaya had me convinced. When you don't take care of your physical health, you're being violent to your body. When you don't nourish the mind and spirit, you are doing a disservice to your inner sanctum. When you allow your mind to fill with negativity and judgment, you darken your being thought by thought. When you fail to protect your emotions against the onslaught of suffering and trauma, you are allowing violence to yourself.

Which will you choose, self-care or self-violence?

In order to further understand the imperative of choosing self-care, let's take a look at what the consequences are of consistently choosing self-violence (the path of self-neglect, self-denial, running on empty, becoming depleted, self-judging, pushing your limits, and saying no to yourself.) There is a price to pay when you live in that space—a price for you and your clients.

CHAPTER 3

OCCUPATIONAL HAZARDS

My sixteen-year-old daughter brought home her boyfriend to meet the folks. This was a momentous night. As we sat around the table, I wanted to hear all about his family in the South, what had brought him to a boarding school in New Hampshire, what his interests were, and so on. Instead, I asked him, "What was your favorite story book when you were growing up?"

Surprised, he thought for a moment, then, answered firmly, "*The Giving Tree.*"

This classic and much beloved book by Shel Silverstein has been around for fifty years. It's the story of a tree and the little boy she loves. Making him happy is what makes her happy. She provides shade and a limb to climb on. When he grows up, she gives him her apples to sell. When he asks for a house, she gives him her branches for lumber. When he is old, he asks for a boat and she offers her trunk. Finally, she is nothing but a stump and the boy, now an elderly man, returns to the tree, rests on her stump, and she is happy.

I have always thought that one's reaction to *The Giving Tree* is something of a Rorschach test. How you interpret it says more about you than about the actual book. It seems that the message is deliberately unclear. Some see the book as a glorious expression of unconditional love or a deeper spiritual statement about how form is impermanent and ultimately irrelevant. Others see it as a commentary on dysfunctional relationships or a message about the dangers of giving and taking too much.

Although my daughter's beau had been comforted by the book's message of sacrificial love, I had always found the story desperately sad.

Now, through the lens of self-care advocate, I can say that the tree most certainly was not taking care of herself. She completely gave herself away and was left with virtually nothing as a result. She gave away her apples, her branches, even her very trunk. In the end, there wasn't much left of that glorious tree.

Clearly, we are all at risk of being proverbial 'stumps' if we continue to give and give and give without concern for replenishment. Fortunately, through the act of self-regeneration, we can create an abundance of resources to share.

BURN OUT

I am not a frequent flyer but when I do fly, I typically keep my head down in a book. Basically introverted, I notice that an open book signals to those around me that I'm not particularly interested in having a conversation. However, a girl has to eat.

So there I was biting into my smoked turkey on honey wheat bread, when the woman next to me began to politely chat about whether Reno, our flight's destination, was my home. *Ugh, caught.* I told her no, I was traveling there on business. As I took another big bite of sandwich I was hoping she might take the hint. But no, she followed with the expected follow-up question, "Oh what kind of business brings you to Reno?"

Sigh. "Actually, I'm headed to Lake Tahoe to speak at a conference. I'm a psychotherapist." Then I thought to myself, *here we go.* Telling someone that I'm a psychotherapist is a conversation starter, conversation killer or the start of a therapy session. Would this woman be intrigued and ask follow-up questions or would she be put off, assuming that I'm going to analyze her? Or, might she bring up her pressing issue of the moment?

What I got was unexpected. "Oh, a therapist." She continued, "I used to be a therapist but I left the field. I completely burned out and now I run a Greek restaurant."

"You burned out?" I blurted. I was fascinated and took my turn to barrage her with questions while she politely tried to hide behind her sandwich.

We ended up having a truly interesting discussion about the hardships of our profession and the dangers of burning out. She revealed that she worked in community mental health for many years and was beaten down by the paperwork, quotas, and red tape. She lost her enthusiasm, vision, and purpose. After her third car accident she knew it was time to exit the profession.

"The Universe kept trying to tell me that something wasn't working in my life. I was always stressed, exhausted, and hanging on by a thread."

I have found that there is burnout (with a small 'b') and there is Burnout (with a big 'B'). Small-b burnout is when you're feeling fried at the end of a long day or an unusually busy week. This is the sort of routine energy depletion that is generally resolved with some relaxation, a good night's sleep, maybe a glass of wine, or perhaps an R&R weekend.

But then, there is big-B burn out, the kind that my flying companion had suffered, which is a deal breaker for your job. Big-B burnout doesn't happen after only a few busy days. It's a chronic condition that arises after the accumulation of months and years of neglect and self-sacrifice. It results from the repetitive wearing down of your mind, body, and spirit.

Robert Wicks, author of *The Resilient Clinician*, provides a comprehensive list of some typical symptoms of big-B chronic burnout. Here are a few of the most common:

- Feeling excessive fatigue—physical and emotional
- Feeling unappreciated, bored, frustrated or angry with your place of work, your clients, your colleagues, your supervisor
- Feeling overwhelmed by your everyday tasks
- Feeling physically ill on a regular basis (headache, stomachache, backache)

The problem is not just personal—it's cultural. We live in a culture where more is better and productivity is king. If you define yourself by how many clients you can see in a day, how many career goals you can achieve, and how many hours you can bill, then big-B burnout is probably in your future.

Recovery requires shifting your mindset and realizing you're worthwhile as a human 'being' and not just as a human 'doing.' And to further bolster your healthier lifestyle choices, micro-self-care practices keep you replenished on a daily basis.

Antidote for burnout: Micro-self-care relaxation practices (Chapter 7)

COMPASSION FATIGUE

I was conducting a family session with two teenage kids and their father, regarding the recent death of their mother/wife. At the end of our very emotional and tenderhearted session, I asked my routine intake closing question. "Do any of you have any questions for me?"

The seventeen-year-old daughter said, "I do." She paused. "How do you listen to stories like ours every day? How do you manage all the feelings and stay sane?"

I smiled. "That's such a good question," I replied. "I have to take really good care of myself so I can keep doing this work."

What I didn't say was, "and if I didn't, then I'd be in a place where I don't care about you or any of my clients."

Let's face it, when you work with suffering every day, you are always at risk of emotional overload. In fact, the tendency and capacity to mimic our clients' emotions are ingrained in our nervous system. Babette Rothschild, in her book *Help for the Helper*, recognizes the growing body of literature that points to mirror neurons in the brain as mechanisms for empathy. One of the functions of mirror neurons is to reflect the emotional content of others and allow us to feel as the other feels. When you feel sad, I feel sad. When I see you feeling anxious, I know how you feel by feeling anxious myself.

According to Rothschild, empathy is an evolved and mostly unconscious process involving both our brain and body. We can take up the emotions and trauma of others without even knowing it. However, imagine a sponge that eventually becomes saturated and can no longer absorb more liquid. We become that saturated sponge if we're not careful. Awareness and intentional self-care are the therapist's best protection from emotional overload.

One of the common and natural defenses against chronic overload is apathy. Not caring acts to numb us, keeping us distant from another's pain. For example, if you work as a social worker in oncology, you might become callous to yet another cancer story. If you work with victims of sexual assault, driven by your feelings of helplessness, you might shut down your emotions at work.

For me, as a grief counselor, loss of my compassionate presence with grievers might look something like, *Oh get over it. Everybody's going to die someday*. Obviously, this wouldn't be a particularly helpful therapeutic stance.

Unfortunately, helpers often wear their compassion fatigue on their sleeves. I'm reminded of a middle aged, overworked doctor I once saw in a New York City clinic. I was in for a shot of some sort and was feeling anxious. Trying to gain some compassionate empathy, I told the doctor that I get anxious about needles. "Tell the nurse," he said without even looking my way as he left the room.

We must dance that precarious tightrope of caring, the delicate balance between accurate empathy and empathic overload. We must be involved in client care but not in their day-to-day lives. We must feel a connection, but not to the detriment of the therapeutic relationship. Sustaining that balance is at once our greatest challenge and our greatest gift. Like the tightrope walker, we must look up to keep our balance. Keeping our eyes on our higher mission helps us keep our balance with our clients.

Antidote for compassion fatigue: Micro-self-care energization practices (Chapter 6)

VICARIOUS TRAUMA

All therapists have traumatic stories that stand out for them: the mother who saw her son's brains blasted on the side of a wall; the husband who walked in on his wife in bed with another man; the father who opened the bedroom door on Christmas morning to find that his son had overdosed on heroin; the mother who kissed the cold lips of her dead baby. Depending on your place of employment and area of specialization, you each have your own traumatic stories of emergency department visits, terminal diagnoses, prison riots, cigarette burn scars, sexual abuse episodes, exploding bombs, and overdose.

As you handle these stories professionally and attempt

to hold them with some degree of distance, you are human nonetheless and are changed by every story you hear. Laura van Dernoot Lipsky and Connie Burk's powerful and paradigm-changing book, *Trauma Stewardship*, is based on the very sound premise that everyone who works with human suffering is inescapably affected by the experience. This, in and of itself, isn't necessarily a problem—ignorance of our susceptibility and denial of our suffering are what lead to the serious and cumulative effects of vicarious trauma. In other words, lack of awareness is the problem, not secondary exposure to trauma itself. If you admit the nature of the beast, you can take appropriate measures to keep yourself well.

Also known as secondary shock or secondary traumatization, vicarious trauma as I use the term here means the actual experience of being exposed to human trauma and suffering, a condition of being a therapist. Essentially, it's in our job description.

My dear colleague Melinda is the first to say that she used to believe that self-care was optional. She thought of it as a luxury, not a necessity. Through years of stress and trauma exposure, though, she was depressed and worn down; she never made self-care a priority. That all changed, however, when she received the diagnosis of stage-3 colon cancer. Months of surgeries, radiation, and chemotherapy left doctors shaking their heads in frustration and doubt. Melinda gained a new awareness of her fragile body and the recognition that it needed a level of care that only she could facilitate. That's when she took on the alternate therapies of supplements, acupuncture, dietary restrictions, and homeopathic remedies. Currently in remission, Melinda is seeing clients again and actively attempts to inspire therapists to see self-care as the number one priority.

"How long do you think you can breathe in noxious fumes without a mask and not be affected?" she asks. She is dedicated to practicing self-care in ways that fortify and cleanse her body, mind, and spirit. She reminds me that self-care could literally be a matter of life and death.

Antidote for vicarious trauma: Micro-self-care grounding practices (Chapter 5)

GOING TO THE BANK

Our work is a bit like going to the bank. We can make daily withdrawals and weekly withdrawals, but if we don't make regular deposits, we're eventually going to go bankrupt. Even overdraft protection only goes so far.

As you can see, with the dangers of burnout, compassion fatigue, and vicarious trauma, we can drain our resources on a consistent basis. That's why self-care deposits—daily deposits, hourly deposits—are truly the only way to keep ourselves vital and healthy. Fortunately, that's where micro-self-care comes to the rescue.

PART II

THE TEMPLATE

CHAPTER 4

PRACTICES FOR A TYPICAL WORKDAY

I HAVE to admit I love being a therapist. I was fortunate to realize my calling to this field when I was twenty-five years old. It felt right immediately. And now, some twenty-five years later, I still feel called to do this work.

My career began in community mental health, and at that time my work days alternated between 9 a.m. to 5 p.m. and 1 to 9 p.m. A workday might have meant getting up early and coming home in time for dinner or getting up later, running errands, and coming home in time for bed. Some days included staff and supervisory meetings, others a back-to-back parade of clients.

Once I had children, I was fortunate to be able to work part-time in private practice, combining what I thought was the best of both worlds. Some days I cancelled clients because I had a child sick at home. Many days, I scheduled sessions so I could be home in time for the school bus. Scattered in between were consultation groups, CEU (Continuing Education Unit) workshops, writing days, and professional conferences.

One of the biggest shifts in my life took place when I remarried and moved to a new home. With children largely grown, I decided to expand my private practice. Likewise, we were planning an addition to our new house to include a separate office with a separate entrance. Though I had never considered working out of my home, it suddenly was possible. So, my previous forty-minute commute was reduced to a twenty second walk downstairs and my typical workday now includes throwing laundry into the washer and taking the dog for a walk. Although this domestic/professional arrangement has its downsides, it has allowed me many freedoms.

One thing is essential, regardless of your work setting, work hours, or office furniture: you need nourishment every single day. As a therapist, just as you need regular nourishing meals to stay healthy and feel well, you need the daily nourishment of micro-self-care to feel grounded, energized, and relaxed. Sometimes, you even need extra helpings.

Have you ever heard (or even preached) the idea that when your stress levels are up, you should spend *more* time taking care of yourself? This makes sense, as stress is a real energy drain. Caring for yourself during times of high stress is analogous to eating extra calories after a workout or having additional communal support after a funeral. Like stress, intense exercise and grieving require extra nourishment. But it isn't always possible to increase your resources for self-care when stress rises. The time and money necessary for traditional avenues of macro-self-care are often exhausted by the crisis at hand.

I experienced this phenomenon when my husband Daniel was diagnosed with colon cancer. After a successful surgery, he began a six-month course of chemotherapy. Dan, at six-feet, five-inches tall, is like a tree. Chemo chopped him down and toppled him over. He couldn't work, often couldn't help around the house, and needed my care, not to mention that the medical bills were excessive.

The good news was that I had the flexibility of private practice and even better, I worked from home. The bad news, clearly, was that my husband had cancer and was incapacitated. I was the sole breadwinner, primary caretaker, chief cook, and bottle washer. My energy requirements and stress response were at an all time high while my resources for macro-self-care were at an all time low. Hobbies, massages, and mini-vacations were not an option. I had to make micro-self-care a daily priority. I had to practice what I preached. I couldn't afford to burn out when I now had added burdens, worries, and responsibilities to manage.

Happily, although we all suffered during those dreary months, my attention to micro-self-care carried me through by increasing my level of awareness, energy, and sanity. I was able to be present with clients and take care of Daniel. I not only survived this crisis, but learned a valuable lesson. I became acutely aware of the importance of daily micro-self-care practices in a profession where exposure to trauma, crisis, negativity, and stress is a daily occurrence.

The point is that micro-self-care is for days of obvious crisis and for days of relative quiet, for busy days and slow days, happy days and sad days. Self-care, like brushing your teeth, is for everyday.

The following section introduces a sampling of ten micro-self-care practices with suggestions on how to weave them through your workday—regardless of your work environment. This chapter offers a balance of different types of practices presented chronologically, from morning to night. You will find:

- A practice to use upon waking
- A practice for starting your workday
- A practice for starting a session
- A practice to use in session, between sessions, and after sessions
- A practice to help you debrief at the end of your workday
- A balance of breath, movement, mindfulness, and visualization practices
- A balance of grounding, energizing, and relaxation practices

Every day may be different but each should have one common denominator: simple self-care.

ALL YOU NEED IS LOVE

What: Generate a feeling of love and connectedness. (This is a grounding practice.)

As you lie in bed in the morning, intentionally imagine breathing in the word (and the feeling) love. As you breathe in the word love, imagine filling yourself with the love that others have for you—love from your spouse, children, grandchildren, pets, best friend. Then, imagine breathing out the word (and the feeling) love. Imagine the love that you have for others just blowing through you—love for your spouse, children, grandchildren, pets, best friend. Be an instrument for breathing in and out a cycle of love.

When: Before you rise from your bed at the start of the day.

Why: There is something to the saying "fake it until you make it." In psychotherapy, religious teachings, medicine, and everyday culture we use imagination and directed behavior to achieve a desired feeling or mood. Consider how we train our children toward an understanding of gratitude by making them say "thank you." Many of the interventions in positive psychology are based on the idea of focusing on life's good aspects. Positive focus leads to positive change. Intentionally imagining a cycle of love not only stimulates feelings of connectedness in the moment but also trains your brain to be more loving and receptive on a regular basis.

My client sat on the couch before me and reached for a tissue. Regina had worked with me many years before, beginning shortly after her two-year-old daughter died. At the time, Regina had two other children, sons ages six and four. However, the death of her youngest, her only girl, felt more than she could bear.

Regina had been told things by others, such as "you have two other children to live for," and "God doesn't give you more than you can handle." Regina felt these platitudes were meaningless and inane. Her beloved child was irreplaceable and no one seemed to understand. For quite a few months she withdrew from her children, husband, and especially her feeling of connection with God. In our work together, she was allowed to grieve deeply and eventually, gradually began to turn her attention back to those who were still living. Now here we were ten years later at the anniversary of Regina's daughter's death. This "angelversary," as we called it, was triggering a strong, emotionally weighted grief reaction.

In general, Regina's life had unfolded well through the years. She and her husband had gotten pregnant again and had twins. Regina felt blessed in many ways and yet never stopped thinking of her perfect baby. She told me she knew she had so much to be grateful for and agreed she was blessed with her husband and four living children. Still, she also felt part of her had died with her baby. Her heart, she said, was like a lump of coal.

I offered several interventions to try to create a shift for her. I suggested she perform a ritual to help her to let go of the heaviest quality of her grief. She created a ritual that involved dropping a bag of rocks to the bottom of a nearby lake, hoping this would release her of her heavy burden. It somewhat helped.

More powerfully, I asked her to work with the idea of letting the "dark chunk" of her heart be filled with more light. She agreed that every morning in bed she would breathe in and breathe out the word love. In the beginning, she concentrated on the love she felt from and for her beloved deceased baby. Over time, she added others to the line-up of love givers and receivers.

Something interesting began to happen for Regina. Her heart image began to shift. When I asked her to describe her heart now, she said it was more like a translucent rose quartz. The effect on her life was also transformative. She could honestly feel the love for her husband and children—she was no longer simply going through the motions.

A heart, from a lump of dark coal to rose quartz. Beautiful.

Reflection: How do you think your days would be different if you filled the vessel of you with love, each and every morning?

CIRCLE OF CARE

What: Connect yourself to your larger community of helpers. (This is an energizing practice.)

Take a circular object and hold it in your hand. You could use a coin, marble, or disc. I have a small quartz circle that I keep in my desk drawer. Hold the object in your hand and say, "I am part of a vast circle of helpers around the globe." As you say this, close your eyes and imagine helpers and healers of all persuasions in your town, state, country, and in countries around the world. Know that you are a part of this vast web of helpers.

When: First thing after you've settled into your office, before you begin your workday activities.

Why: By the nature of our work, we are often isolated. Whether we work in private practice, in a clinic, or some other setting, at some point we close our doors and are alone with our clients. It can be easy to feel alone in our endeavors. If there is one thing that all of psychology can agree on it is that relationships are crucial. We are relational beings. From our neurology, biology, and body chemistry to our attachment systems, moods, drives, and thought processes, we are formed, moved, and responsive to other people. This brief technique reminds us that we are part of a web of healers and helpers around the world.

When I first became licensed, I felt privileged and excited to have entered the field of helping professionals. I remember that whenever I travelled to a new town, I got a thrill out of looking at the yellow pages (yes, this was long before the internet). The "counselors" and "psychotherapists" sections were always huge. I felt a little elation knowing I was one of them; I was in their club.

I even remember when I purchased my own quarter-inch advertisement in my town's phonebook. What fun to see the new annual edition arrive.

There are many ways to summon that sense of connection, of being one of the gang. Often when I hold my quartz disc in the morning, I imagine therapists that I have consulted through the years, friends who are therapists, or colleagues that I have met at conferences. I imagine therapists sitting in their offices in far-flung states and countries, doing their best to be of service.

I imagine shamans, wise elders, and healers in other cultures. I imagine healers in countries where I have visited (Bali, India, China) and continents I haven't (South America, Africa, Australia).

I also get a kick out of imagining fictional therapists. Think of the imaginary therapists you have seen in books, movies, and television shows. Some of my personal favorites include:

- Richard Dreyfuss's character Dr. Leo Marvin, a therapist and author plagued by his intrusive patient Bob, played by Bill Murray in the film *What About Bob?*
- Barbra Streisand's character Susan Lowenstein, a therapist who falls in love with her patient's brother, played by Nick Nolte in the film *The Prince of Tides.*

- Barbra Streisand, again, who plays a hilarious sex therapist married to Dustin Hoffman in the film *Meet the Fockers*.
- Billy Crystal's character Ben Sobel, therapist to a mafia boss, played by Robert De Niro in the films *Analyze This* and *Analyze That*.
- Steve Carell's character Dr. Bernie Feld, a couples counselor to Merrill Streep and Tommy Lee Jones in the film *Hope Springs*.
- Robin Williams's character Dr. Sean Maguire, a compassionate therapist to the brilliant but troubled adolescent played by Matt Damon in the film *Good Will Hunting*.
- Gabriel Byrne's character Dr. Paul Weston, who takes us through the intimate world of psychotherapy, session by session, in the HBO series *In Treatment*.

So whether you conjure up factual or fictional therapists, think of them and put yourself in the grand circle of helpers around the world who have made a difference since the dawn of time. From ancient medicine men to Freud and to the present moment—you're part of the tribe.

Reflection: How do you feel when you know that you're part of something larger than yourself?

DOORKNOB CONFESSION

What: Connect to your larger purpose. (This is an energizing practice.)

Think to yourself, "I do this work because ______." Maybe you do your work because you want to alleviate suffering, help people, understand yourself better, make a difference in the world, or because it is interesting. Get in touch with your motivation before each and every client encounter.

When: As you put your hand on the doorknob to open the door and welcome in your client.

Why: Most of us forget what propelled us into this career in the first place. That initial motivation may still be the primary glue keeping you to the field. Or perhaps different motivations have surfaced through the years. Whatever it is, something is inspiring you to do this work. It's too easy to get bogged down by the day-to-day realities of our jobs, especially if we lose sight of our purpose. Van Dernoot Lipsky and Burk (2009) stress the value of reflecting daily on the question, "Why am I doing what I am doing?" Ready awareness of our purpose is a powerful antidote to feelings of helplessness that come with trauma exposure. Placing your primary motivation front and center in your mind with the turning of the doorknob initiates a sense of purpose before each client.

After Daniel and I got married, Daniel realized that his academic career in archeology—was not a good fit for us. The desirable positions in his specialty called him to another country but both of us were tied to the joint custody of our five children.

What to do? He considered teaching as a possibility, but in the meantime began to manage my private psychotherapy practice. I remember the conversation with him when he said, "You know, what I'd really like to do is what you do. I want to be a therapist."

My first response was, "No way—you can't go to graduate school (again)!" My second response was, "Why?"

He saw that the work was meaningful. He was interested in the emotional lives of people. He saw that we could dovetail our careers and eventually work together. He sensed that he would be good at it.

And so, Daniel went back to school in mental health counseling. During one of his initial classes, he had to write a paper on what had inspired him to become a counselor. The students shared in class their reasons for entering the field.

One woman was motivated to help children in abusive homes since she had suffered a similar fate as a child. One man wanted to help addicts in recovery since he had been helped by the system. One woman said she wanted to make a difference in people's lives on the deepest level. Another reported that her personality simply lent itself to being a compassionate listener.

Dan asked me what had led me to social work school when I was twenty-five years old.

"I haven't thought of that in years," I replied.

"Well," Dan volunteered, "my teacher said that we should keep our purpose fresh in our heads. People who burn out are those who lose touch with their dreams and motivations."

I was reminded that I needed to keep my purpose front and center every single workday. And what better reminder than the infamous doorknob.

Rather than wait for the stereotypical end-session confession ("Oh by the way, this is my last session . . ." "Did I mention that my mother sexually abused me?" "I think I'm going to ask Charles for a divorce.") I offer my own before-session confession as I reach for the doorknob: "I'm doing this work because I'm called to help people in emotional pain." It's the motivation that led me into the field all those years ago and it's still the motivation that keeps me doing this work now.

Yes. Let me remember.

Reflection: Do you remember what drove you into the field? Has your purpose changed? Can you find that seed of inspiration and make it relevant today?

HARK HOW THE BELLS

What: Create a mindful moment for you and your client. (This is a grounding practice.)

Ring a Tibetan singing bowl (or other chime) three times with your client. Listen to the sound as it dissipates into the air around you and then begin the session.

When: At the start of a session.

Why: This is a mindfulness-based ritual that helps you and your client transition to your time together. Focusing attention on the sound of the bell helps the client leave the energy of out-in-the-world and enter the sanctuary of in-the-session. This practice helps both therapist and client's mind and body to settle into the session and prepare the way for whatever needs to arise. Dan Siegel, in his book, *The Mindful Therapist*, reminds us that mindful awareness not only offers us resilience in the face of uncertainty and challenge but also is a crucial determinant in our ability to help others.

Researching material for my book, *Shortcuts to Inner Peace*, I was steeped in various mindfulness materials. I went to workshops and gathered CEU's that were focused on mindfulness. I read books on mindfulness. And I listened to countless free webinars on mindfulness.

I had pages and pages of notes on this simple practice of focused, nonjudgmental awareness. I began to delve into the subtle lessons of acceptance, openness, willingness, and compassion that were embedded in the broad concept of mindfulness.

However, it was during a talk about attention by Gregg Krech, author of *A Natural Approach to Mental Awareness*, when a thought occurred to me. He was talking about how the Zen monk and prolific writer, Ticht Naht Hahn, uses bells at his monasteries as a way of creating intentional moments of mindfulness. At the sound of a bell, monks and practitioners pause and take three conscious breaths. Greg shared that whenever he hears a phone ring, he pauses a moment before answering. He is inspired to be mindful upon hearing any bell or electronic ring.

That's when I asked myself, *How can I use a bell in my workday to center myself? What if I actually rang a bell with a client so that we could be mindful together?*

I have always loved bells but especially Tibetan singing bowls, so I went online and ordered a small brass bowl. It felt like a precious artifact in my New Hampshire office. Years later, I had the good fortune to travel to a Tibetan village in Dharamsala, India and was amazed to find Tibetan singing bowls for sale on practically every corner.

Once my clients learned to expect the bell ritual at the beginning of session, neither of us could go without it. These are the words that I say: "Let's start with the bell." (Then we both—or all of us, if I'm working with a couple or family—close our eyes.) "Notice your breath, breathing in and breathing out. Feel your body relaxing and settling into the couch. Allow yourself to arrive into this space, into this moment. When you hear the sound of the bell, let the sound calm you. Let it relax you. And let the tone take you deeper and deeper within to a place of spacious stillness. Breathe in the bell." I then ring the bell three slow, consecutive times.

This calming ritual now feels an essential starting point for a session. It helps me center, orient myself, and prepare to be an instrument for help and healing. Clients find it calms them from whatever busy energy brought them to my office.

I have had clients tell me they've bought their own bell to ring at home. I was also once chastised by a client when I was willing to skip the ritual. This particular client, thirty minutes late for a session, came running breathlessly into the room and plopped onto the couch. "Sorry I'm late," she said.

"Since we don't have much time together today," I responded, "maybe we should just skip the bell and move onto our session."

"Oh no," she intoned. "If nothing else, I need the bell! In fact, I need a double bell!" And so we had a double bell. She was right—I needed it too. Lesson learned: I never suggested skipping the bell again.

Reflection: How do you act differently as a therapist when you begin each session from a place of centered mindful awareness?

FOOTLOOSE

What: Regain your awareness by grounding to the earth. (This is a grounding practice.)

Put both feet on the floor, press your toes down, and imagine breathing in and out through the soles of your feet. Next, imagine strength and energy from the earth moving up through your feet and upwards through your spine. Breathe it in.

When: When you find yourself reacting to a loud, agitated, or angry client. Or anytime you find yourself internalizing your client's experience and losing touch with the context of the room.

Why: Getting stuck in your head or caught up in your own emotions can happen to novices in the field as well as the most experienced therapists. Whether it is your own countertransference coming up or a case of somatic empathy, when your internal experience takes over, you lose clarity of your external awareness and may feel disconnected. As Rothschild emphasizes, dual awareness of our internal and external experience is essential for therapeutic clarity. "Footloose" combines a shift in body posture with imagery to quickly ground you in the context of your external world.

"Stop interrupting me," Grace said loudly and harshly. She was virtually bellowing at her husband who simply laughed in her face. This laugh only served to enrage her. "You are an ignorant bully and I *hate* you."

Grace's amygdala (her fight/flight/freeze response) was activated. She sat right in front of me on the edge of her chair. Glaring at me, flushed, and shaking she said, "Do you see what I have to put up with?"

He countered, more quietly but with a snide tone, "And do you see what *I* have to put up with?"

This old married couple could have been two four-year-olds. They had been together for forty-one years, and now Grace wanted to leave the marriage. She suspected her husband of having an affair.

Grace suddenly burst into tears and, Al, in an obvious state of discomfort, started snickering. Grace looked at him and yelled, "You're an idiot!"

I love working with couples, even couples in serious distress. Yet, there are still some days when I feel myself lost in the fray. In this session with Grace and Al, as I witnessed two grown people behaving so callously with one another, I felt my heart beat a little faster and noticed in myself a growing distance from the interactions in the room. As therapists, we often see the most tender, sacred, and vulnerable underbelly of human nature. We also see its brutal and insensitive claws.

I felt agitated and was losing touch with my experience, confidence, and compassion. I could feel my body tension mimicking theirs. Various thoughts ran through my head: *What the heck do I do now? I haven't the slightest idea how to help them. Could they become violent? When will this session be over?*

Immediately, I uncrossed my legs and placed both feet firmly on the floor. Imagining my breath moving through the souls of my feet to and from the earth below, I noticed the pace of my breath slow and my awareness stabilize. I became grounded.

Exhaling calmly, I said to Grace, "Let me help you dial down the energy," and I made a slow, wide turning motion with my right hand, as if turning an old fashioned television dial. Dropping her shoulders, she took the cue, clearly relieved to let go of some of her tension. Perhaps she sensed my relaxed posture and groundedness.

I'd like to say that the rest of the session unfolded perfectly, that Al was able to connect with the loneliness and fear below Grace's anger and blame, and that Grace was able to see the sadness and helplessness behind Al's cynicism and emotional distance.

But no. They both remained activated: Grace rushing forward to be heard, and Al moving farther away.

The good news is that I kept myself grounded during the storm. They were blinded by the dark clouds and rain while I, playing ground control, stayed safely on land.

Reflection: How many times a day does your clients' reactivity threaten to take you into their chaos?

GO IN PEACE

What: Send good will to your clients as they leave the session. (This is a relaxation practice.)

Put your hand on your heart and then hold it out to the universe. Say or think the words, "May you go in peace and may you be free from suffering."

When: After your client exits and you have closed the door behind them.

Why: Spreading good will has a way of opening your heart. Especially for clients whose stories you tend to carry with too much weight, sending them off with well wishes offers the effect of clearing your own emotional space and transitioning to your next client or activity. Much as the Tibetan prayer wheels or flags spread good will through the air, this practice also is about spreading the seeds of goodness and peace.

I conducted a brief phone-screening interview with Janice, a sixty-six year old woman who wanted to come to session to determine whether or not she should stay in her marriage. We made an appointment for later in the week.

As she arrived and sat on the couch, she immediately opened the session with the words, "I already know that I want to stay married but I just want Frank to quit pestering me about sex."

I asked her to backtrack and tell me about her relationship with Frank, her husband of thirty years. She described him as lazy, rude, a drinker, a slob, and as clueless. The problem was that she had stopped having sex with him about six months ago and now he wasn't acting quite as clueless.

"What do you mean?" I asked.

She quipped, "*Now* he wants to talk about the relationship. He wants to talk about what's wrong, what he can do to make things better, and how we can start up our sex life again."

"You're not interested in that?" I inquired.

"Heaven's, no . . ." she jumped in. "I don't want to have sex anymore, ever. Not with him and not with anyone."

"So let me get this straight," I summarized. "You don't want to have sex with your husband or work on your relationship but you don't want to divorce him either. You just want him to quit bothering you?"

"That's pretty much it," she reflected.

I paused for a moment, thinking, *Well, what would you like my help with?*

"I was hoping you could see me and Frank together and tell him that we're fine just like this. Maybe tell him that it's healthy to stop having sex at our age," she said.

"Well," I said slowly, "that might not be true for Frank. I'd be happy to see you both together and work with you to understand what's going on." She snorted and shook her head 'no.'

She added, "I just want him to leave things alone."

"You know," I continued, "my hands are really tied. As a counselor, it's not my job to convince Frank that a sexless marriage is in his best interest."

Janice said, emphatically, "Well then I guess I wasted my time in coming here today."

Yes, it did seem so. I tried to help her explore her relationship with Frank, concerns about intimacy, and fears about getting divorced. In the end, she wanted none of that. Unfortunately, I couldn't help her with her goal. By the end of the session, it was clear that we would most likely never see each other again.

Once I closed the door behind her, I had a spontaneous desire to wish her well. I extended out my hand, blew along it, as if blowing a feather off my palm, and chanted, "Go now in peace. Be well."

I found the gesture so calming that I adopted the practice after I close the door behind all of my clients. I blow them a breath of peace and wish them well. In the process, I find myself relaxing into the moment of goodbye, whether I plan to see them next week or never again.

Reflection: How do you feel when you open your heart and send good will toward another being?

COAT SLEEVES

What: Invigorate yourself. (This is an energizing practice.)

Stand up and swing your arms to the right and left. Twist the core of your body from one side to the other letting your arms add momentum. Allow each arm to flap to the alternate side of your body as you twist from side to side.

When: In between clients.

Why: This practice of a spinal twist releases energy, and rebalances your awareness. This energetic movement brings you out of a post-session bias towards inner awareness by awakening your external sensory organs. "Without dual awareness," writes Rothschild, "clear thinking is not possible" (2006, p. 175). Dual awareness refers to the simultaneous reception of external circumstances and internal feelings. It is essential for the therapist to retain a balance between empathy and groundedness, internal and external awareness. This tool brings you back to a place of balance.

There were four of us. Our consultation group consisted of a social worker, psychologist, marriage and family counselor, and mental health counselor. We were a sampling of the primary mental health disciplines.

We had been together for almost ten years. While we shared cases, conferred on CEU workshops, and consulted on professional dilemmas, our primary consultation purpose was to support each other. We had been through a divorce, a remarriage, multiple child launchings, and even a few grandchildren.

We had been through surgeries, medical emergencies, and deaths of family members not to mention the important tasks of sharing book and film recommendations.

When I asked if we could brainstorm about therapist self-care, my colleagues were only too happy to oblige. Without question, these women were dedicated to their healthy lifestyles of good diet, regular exercise, meditation practices, and social networks.

Then, Rachel said, "Actually, for me, professional self-care basically boils down to good business practices."

"What do you mean?" we chimed in.

"Well, I don't email clients on weekends." We all nodded. I was thinking the word *boundaries*.

"And," she continued, "I don't get more than one day behind on my session notes or charts." We all nodded again. I was thinking the words *time management*.

"And of course," she lowered her voice, "I *never* see more than five clients in a day. It's my personal limit."

I knew what she meant but I also knew that she was voicing a private practice luxury. I remember working in a clinic where we were expected to see eight clients a day, every day. That meant booking nine in a day, allowing for the inevitable cancellation.

But Shannon, also in private practice, said, "I often see eight clients a day."

We looked at her incredulously. All these years and we knew she carried a high caseload, but eight clients a day? *By choice?* I thought. All three of us looked at her with our mouths gaping.

"I like my house and I have to pay the mortgage. I don't want to move," she said emphatically.

"But how do you do it? How do you keep yourself replenished with such an intense client schedule?"

"Coat sleeves," she replied simply. "Empty coat sleeves."

We stared at her, waiting for the punch line. So she stood up and demonstrated this magical technique, which she assured us was sure to clear and restore energy between client sessions. She stood before us and swung her arms from right to left. Spontaneously, the rest of us stood up and started twisting our bodies to the right and left, our empty coat sleeves slapping from side to side. We laughed at our silliness.

Although initially skeptical, I have since frequently used the coat sleeves technique between clients. It wakes up my senses and creates a feeling of fresh energy.

Reflection: Have you ever felt sorry for your last client of the day because you know they are getting the dregs of your therapeutic abilities?

BUBBLE TEA

What: Give yourself a moment of rejuvenation and self-renewal with an afternoon beverage. (This is a relaxation practice.)

Pick your favorite beverage (tea, coffee, water, juice, and so on) and spend three to five minutes doing nothing else but drinking your beverage. Let yourself be in a bubble of being rather than doing. Feel the temperature of the cup in your hand. Smell the fragrance. Feel the liquid going down your throat. Gaze out a window. You can even set the timer on your phone as a way to define and protect your few moments of peace. Allow yourself this respite.

When: In the afternoon.

Why: We all feel better and perform better when we allow ourselves to rest. Nobody does good work with a dull saw. In fact, self-renewal, or 'sharpening the saw' is the seventh habit of Stephen Covey's popular book, *The 7 Habits of Highly Effective People*. Covey's seventh habit champions the idea, as I do in this book, that self-rejuvenation is essential to well-being, mental health, and a life of balance. As I've pointed out before, for a therapist, self-renewal is an ethical obligation; as a 'dull' saw, you will harm your clients (or at the very least, you will be less effective).

If you cannot take a long break, carve out three to five minutes. It will be something of a shock at first to do nothing while you sip. You will be tempted to check email, browse through a magazine, return phone calls, or even journal. Instead, stay with the relatively unusual feeling of doing nothing, mindfully taking in the sensations of the tea. You will feel rejuvenated in a relatively short amount of time. Create a bubble of just being and take your beverage without doing anything productive—restoring your balance is productive enough.

I was having lunch with a colleague and we were talking about self-care practices. Susan took her self-care very seriously. If she didn't, she told me, she would be a terrible therapist.

She explained to me that she exercised religiously. She always made time on the weekends for fun. She never saw more than four clients in a day. She had a weekly date with her husband (she was an empty nester). Then, she leaned toward me conspiratorially, "But my favorite self-care practice is that every day, between 3 and 3:30 p.m., I have a cup of tea and a square of extra dark chocolate."

She always schedules her clients around this ritual and never breaks it. She enjoys every aspect of boiling the tea, selecting the tea, steeping it, pouring it, drinking it (not to mention the chocolate indulgence). She added, "I look forward to that take-me-away moment all day long! I know it's just for me."

As she spoke, I was reminded of two classic rituals: Japanese tea ceremonies, and the monastic practice of simply drinking tea when drinking tea. The art and awe that surround these intentional practices take mindfulness to an art form.

When I was on my first silent retreat in an Episcopal monastery, I had brought a stack of reading materials, writing ideas, prayer lists, and so on. The brother who brought me to my room said, "Might I suggest that while you're here, don't bother with too many activities, spiritual or otherwise. Drink a cup of tea and while you're drinking it, *just* drink the tea—do nothing else." It sounded simple at the time but it was surprisingly difficult to do in an era that glorifies multi-tasking. Yet, I've found that the break offered by this simple ritual is downright healing.

Work will always present itself and yes, it will be there when you're done with your tea. So, protect that private bubble of stillness and rest in the space.

Reflection: Notice how you feel after a short, silent break. You are worth it.

PUNCH OUT POSITIVE

What: Counteract your negativity bias with a positive debriefing. (This is an energizing practice.)

Take a reflective moment and mentally list three things that went well today. Your reflections might include: a pivotal moment in a session, successful intake, positive interaction with a colleague, supportive word from a supervisor, or an email with good news. As you reflect on each experience, take ten to twenty extra seconds to hold, expand, breathe in, and absorb the positive feelings.

When: At the end of your workday, before you leave the office.

Why: This tool is a kind of debriefing exercise that helps you reflect positively on your day. In *Hardwiring Happiness*, Rick Hanson emphasizes the human brain's negativity bias. Because of this tendency, our minds are more adept at highlighting our negative experiences than our positive ones. Hanson's antidote, an exercise he calls "taking in the good," helps imprint positive experiences and create neural pathways of happiness by staying with positive feelings. Take a moment at the close of your workday to spotlight the positive and reinforce what went right in your day.

"Today, pay attention to the color blue." I read this in my monthly calendar of exercises.

I was taking a distance class through the ToDo Institute on the power of attention in one's life. Each day of the month had a different directive to help us sharpen our powers of attention.

I had paid attention to sounds, light, shadows, and smiles. But paying attention to blue changed my whole perspective. That day, I was taken aback by the intensity of the azure sky. *Hey*, I thought, *I never noticed that blue mailbox down the street.* Blue popped out of every storefront, window, and bookcase. I saw blue everywhere.

Our minds become what they rest upon. This is the promise (and the danger) of neuroplasticity. And that is why we especially want to take advantage of *self-directed* neuroplasticity. This means choosing the focus of our attention—choosing what our minds rest upon is essentially choosing what our minds will become.

Hanson is especially skilled at describing the advantages of taking in the good. He uses the acronym HEAL to lay it out in steps:

Have a good experience (or notice that you've had one)
Enrich the experience (by holding, expanding, and feeling it anew)
Absorb the experience (imagine you are a sponge pulling the experience into you)
Link the experience (let this positive experience/feeling overlay a negative)

Hanson also writes about the importance of turning a fact into an experience. For example, if one of your good facts of the day was, "I had an excellent intake and I know I can help this client," in your end-day reflection, you should allow yourself to feel the experience of being helpful. Let yourself soak up that good experience of excellence. Notice the sensory impressions you remember from the intake and know in your bones that you're going to be helpful.

Most positive moments are wasted on the brain. That is, they don't sink in and thus don't create happy neural networks. When you punch-out positive, you debrief from your day, shift your attention to what went well, and imprint the experience to the benefit your brain. Win, win, and win.

Reflection: Is it difficult for you to notice what went well in your day?

RESET

What: Relax your mind and body with the 4–7-8 breath. (This is a relaxation practice.)

Inhale through your nose to the count of four. Hold your breath to the count of seven. Then exhale through your mouth, as if you are blowing air out through a straw, to the count of eight. Repeat the cycle two more times.

When: While driving to and from work.

Why: Dr. Andrew Weil teaches this ancient breathing technique, which calms and recalibrates the central nervous system. Releasing an exhale that is twice as long as an inhale has an immediate effect on the parasympathetic nervous system (PSN). You can think of the PSN as the brakes on your stress response. When practicing this breath regularly, over time, the effect is a calmer, less reactive disposition.

It started with her fingers shaking. Then her hands began to shake. Next her arms and feet started tapping. Within a few moments she was trembling like a leaf, from head to toe.

Aleisha was in such a state because she was upset with her husband. You see, they had suffered one of the worst events that a couple can endure: the death of a child. Clark had been home alone with their four-year-old daughter on the night that Samantha choked to death on a grape.

This tragedy was terrible enough in and of itself but it was also ripping Aleisha and Clark apart. Aleisha blamed Clark for being negligent, not cutting the grapes into pieces, not being successful with the Heimlich maneuver, not calling the ambulance sooner. She believed that Samantha might still be alive if she had been home that night. Aleisha conjured a litany of blame to avoid the fact that nothing could bring Samantha back.

As I listened to Aleisha and watched her body shaking, I commented, "Can you tell me what you're feeling in your body?"

She wrung her hands together and said, "Oh, I'm sorry . . . this shaking, it always happens when I get upset." Just saying this caused her to shake all the more.

I assured her there was no need to be sorry but wondered if she'd like to learn a technique that could calm her in this moment. She did, and so I led all three of us in a session of the 4–7-8 breath.

Afterwards, she was visibly more relaxed. The intense shaking had scaled back to a minor shaking and within a few moments, even that subsided. She agreed to use this tool daily.

I use the 4–7-8 breath regularly and began doing this when I discovered it helped with nerves before giving a presentation at a conference.

Aleisha has a long way to go in letting her anger evaporate so she can get to the sorrow underneath, but this tool will help her deactivate so she can start to connect with Clark in her pain.

Reflection: What self-soothing techniques do you use to activate your nervous system's 'rest and digest' response?

PART III

THE RESOURCES

CHAPTER 5

PRACTICES FOR GROUNDING

Once was enough for me. One hot air balloon ride in my lifetime was quite sufficient. While trying to enjoy the natural beauty of Utah's mountains, I found myself nervous, distracted, displaced, and scattered. I was so disconcerted by the mechanics of my hot air lifeline, I practically missed the entire aerial perspective.

When I finally got back to the grassy field, I breathed a sigh of relief. Grounded, I felt anchored and firmly rooted back into the present moment. My feelings of safety and centeredness slowly returned. Although being grounded might mean different things to different people, in this book I am using the term to mean a feeling of being focused, anchored in the immediate environment, and safe in the present moment.

"Isn't that mindfulness?" you might ask.

Certainly, there are aspects of mindfulness in the experience of being grounded. However, mindfulness, strictly speaking, is a kind of nonjudgmental awareness of your present circumstances, regardless of the experience. You could, for example, be quite mindfully aware of being angry or distant. You could be mindful of being frightened or grief stricken.

Groundedness, on the other hand, is the state of feeling unshaken to the core, having your wits about you, and being rooted in your purpose. Picture a solid oak, firm in the midst of a raging storm. Picture the hot air balloon tethered to the ground, no longer at the mercy of the wind.

Being grounded reduces your reactivity and is characterized by a strengthened dual awareness that keeps you from getting hijacked by your emotions. While at work, mindful of your blissful strength, you radiate a sense of tranquility and confidence to your client. Grounding, for each of us, creates the firm base that allows us to guard against vicarious trauma, keep perspective around counter-transference, and do our work well. To the degree that we lose groundedness, we become susceptible to the currents of our clients' emotions and our own vulnerabilities.

It is in the face of our most challenging clients that our ability to stay grounded is tested. For me, this client was Karen Perry. Karen provided her consent for me to use her real name because she is, in fact, a very public figure as a result of her terrible tragedy. She has chosen to share her story in a variety of ways as her means of transcending her grief.

It was Thanksgiving Eve 2011 when I saw the breaking news. A private plane in Phoenix, Arizona had crashed into Superstition Mountain, killing all eight people aboard. This news was tragic enough, of course, but the tragedy somehow intensified when details emerged that all three of Karen's children (ages ten, eight and six) had died aboard that plane (along with their dad, Karen's ex-husband).

Having worked with hundreds of bereaved parents, I can attest that the loss of a child is one of the most dreadful, painful, and deeply searing losses imaginable. While it's unbearable enough to lose one child, losing more than one feels unspeakable. But to lose three—your only three—is unthinkable. My heart went out to this woman.

To my surprise, four months later, in March 2012, I received an email from Karen. She told me she had read my book, *Transcending Loss*, and been helped by it. She wanted to know if she could work with me. There was only one problem. She lived in Arizona and I lived in New Hampshire. Fortunately, there was Skype video.

And so, it came to pass that Karen became my first Skype client.

I was nervous before our first session—nervous about the technology, trying to make a therapeutic connection through cyberspace, the magnitude of her loss, and what I might possibly say that would make a difference. In fact, I felt blown away by the immensity of her tragic situation. I recognized that if I was going to be able to hear Karen without my own issues getting in the way, I needed to be intentional about grounding myself. Even before I accepted her Skype call, I began gripping the floor with my toes and imagined I was breathing through my feet, staying connected to the ground.

"Footloose" (Chapter 4) was my go-to practice as I entered my session with Karen.

Our first session was a success and she asked to continue to work with me. As I met with her over the course of the next fifteen months, I learned that Karen was an amazingly brave and resilient woman. She hadn't just faced the loss of her children, she had survived a multitude of challenges in her lifetime, including life-threatening illness, bitter divorces, financial stresses, and children with special needs.

During our first year of working together, I companioned Karen as she experienced the first year of birthdays and holidays without her children. I listened as she told me about climbing the mountain to the crash site on the anniversary of their deaths. I agonized with her as she reviewed photos and mementos of their lives. I asked questions after she consulted psychics and mediums. I always felt that Karen taught me more about resilience than I could ever teach her.

And then one day, Karen mentioned to me that she had been approached by OWN (the Oprah Winfrey Network) for a new program about tragedy and transformation called *In Deep Shift*. She asked if I would be willing to chat with them and participate in the segment. Before I knew it, I was on my way to Phoenix to be filmed with Karen.

And so it came to pass that Karen was my first client with whom I ever recorded a session for television.

As I came into the sweltering summer heat of Phoenix, I found myself feeling lost in the business of travel and feeling shaken by the anxiety of bringing our therapeutic relationship before cameras. I filled my morning in the hotel room with personal grounding practices: I started with a body scan (Tether Ball, p. 000), followed by a positive visualization (Imagine That, p. 000), and ended with a brief meditation (ABC p. 000). By the time the camera crew picked me up to take me to Karen's house, I felt grounded in a feeling of confidence and rooted in my sense of purpose.

When Karen and I finally met, we hugged; we cried; we held hands. She walked me into her home and showed me photographs of the children. We sat in her kitchen, talking like old friends, all the while being filmed for television. The entire scene had a surreal quality to it.

Finally, a crew of five filmed us in session together on Karen's back deck. You might think there could be nothing authentic about a session under bright lights and in front of cameras. There was the almost unbearable summer heat, the onlookers, her dog, airplanes overhead, pauses in filming—how could anything therapeutic occur? But, to my surprise, the experience was amazing. The mountains, the very mountains that claimed her children, were visible to us as we spoke. Feeling myself grounded and confident in my ability to stay focused on Karen, I was able to share with her my sense of calm and safety. The strength of our therapeutic relationship was able to shine through and Karen and I fell into the comfortable pattern of our practiced working dynamic.

With Karen, I ventured into new territory over and over again—complex clinical issues, cyberspace technology, cross country travel, a home visit, in-session television recording, and conversations with film techies, producers, and the show host. I broke several boundaries that I had always held firm as a therapist. With Karen, I let my soul touch and be touched by a woman who had experienced more sorrow in her lifetime than I could ever imagine. With Karen, I learned to ground myself in order to show up for what was being asked of me.

NOT EVERY client will present the challenges and opportunities that Karen Perry offered me—but they will present with a unique story. They will have dreams, expectations, hopes, and sorrows to share. If you're not grounded in the process, you will be knocked off course. You will be pulled into their stories; you will internalize their emotions; you will suffer their pain as surely as if you were being yanked through the looking glass and down the rabbit hole.

Grounding practices stabilize your awareness even when you're feeling weak. They keep you centered, even when you feel unsure. They keep you anchored so that you're not swept away by the tides of trauma, sorrow, and human suffering that you encounter. The practices offered in this section will keep you grounded in the moment with a strong sense of your inner strength and equanimity.

GOOD DAY

What: Set a positive intention for your day.

State an intention in the present tense, as if it's already happening. Say, "Today, I am open to joy." Or "Today, I treat myself with respect and loving kindness." Or "Today I am a pioneer of self-care!" Or "Today I am filled with gratitude for the blessings in my life." Don't check your phone first thing or jump up in a panic. Spend at least a minute breathing in your daily intention. "I am gracious as my day unfolds." "I am rooted in joy." For added power, write it down on a piece of paper and keep it where you can see it during the day.

When: In your bed, before you get up in the morning.

Why: Setting an intention is a powerful practice. James Baraz, in *Awakening Joy*, claims that setting a morning intention has the power to "incline the mind" in a certain direction. Our minds are powerful yet easily manipulated. The early moments of the morning are a particularly receptive time to program the mind for the day ahead. Use this practice to come out of your dream world and bring awareness to your body, emotions, and daily intention.

Joseph was new to therapy but, out of desperation, had sought help in learning some stress management skills. He was not only grinding his teeth at night but his physician had read him the riot act on the dangerous effects of stress on his health. His recent high blood pressure results indicated that he needed to make some serious changes in his life.

I asked him to tell me about a typical day in his life. "Well," he said, "my alarm goes off, I check my email, and then I'm off to the races."

"You check your email? Right after you get up?" I asked, confused.

"Heck no," he said. "I use my phone as my alarm clock and so I check my email while I'm still in bed, before I even get up to pee."

I think it's time to change that habit, I thought to myself.

The first few moments of waking up are an important part of the day. Just as what you eat for breakfast can make or break your morning energy level, the first few thoughts have a major impact on the trajectory of your day. The dreamy minutes between sleep and wakefulness are when the mind is especially suggestible and ripe for hypnotic suggestion.

However, most of us tend to scan and prepare for our day ahead, orienting ourselves to what is coming up. Is it the weekend, a workday? Is the day ahead expected to be easy or challenging? Do you have an especially problematic client today? Is your schedule packed? Turning your immediate attention to your problems, challenges, emails, and to-do lists is like putting your stress on steroids.

Whether your day is one of work, leisure, stress, or fun, when you set your daily intention with words that evoke tender replenishment and positive self-regard, you set the tone for the day and ready yourself to handle daily circumstances with compassion and equanimity.

The thoughts that start your day matter. Make them count.

Reflection: What kind of day do you create with your morning thoughts?

HUGS AND KISSES

What: Comfort yourself with an embrace.

Wrap your arms around yourself. Close your eyes and squeeze your body tightly for ten to twenty seconds. For extra emphasis, imagine yourself as a young child and imagine hugging your younger self. As an extra bonus, as you hug yourself create bilateral stimulation by alternately tapping one shoulder and then the other, for up to thirty taps.

When: When you are feeling anxious or unsettled before, during, or after a session. Use this particularly if you feel you failed your client.

Why: The self-embrace combined with alternate shoulder tapping, called the "Butterfly Hug," was first devised as a modified EMDR intervention by counselors working with traumatized children after the 1998 earthquake in Mexico City. The bilateral stimulation triggers a soothing effect in the brain and body.

We are wired to respond to touch. Psychologist, Kelly McGonigal, author of *Yoga for Pain Relief*, reflects on the simple act of offering a hug to yourself. Citing a study that demonstrated that self-hugging acts to reduce physical pain, Kelly writes, "A self-hug should reduce pain in other ways, too, providing contact comfort and a feeling of safety and self-compassion that reduces the nervous system's reactivity to pain and threat" (2011).

If you've never seen the movie *Temple Grandin*, then run don't walk to view it. Starring Clare Danes in one of her quieter roles, it is the true-life story of an autistic woman who made her way through high school, college, and graduate school, specializing in animal behavior as a consultant to the livestock industry. She is now a professor and animal rights activist, as well as an advocate for autism awareness.

According to her autobiographical movie, Temple spent some summers on her aunt's farm where she watched cows led into a tight pen. As each cow mooed in distress, the walls of the metal pen closed in to gently squeeze the cow. A metal hug. The cows were immediately calmed.

As Temple watched this, she was intrigued. She wondered if she could create a contraption that would offer her a similar calming squeeze. Using her brilliant scientific mind, she created a "squeeze machine" while in college. She tested this machine by conducting a research study to determine its effects on college students. She demonstrated that the machine stimulated a calming response in even those without autism.

The film shows several moving scenes in which Temple is overcome with anxiety. Rather than engage in more typical autistic self-soothing behaviors, she headed for her squeeze machine. She claimed that the machine created a necessary corrective emotional and neurological experience for her, helping her to become more social, interactive, and tolerant of physical touch from humans. Not only was the squeeze comfortable and relaxing, it was healing. In the end, she credited the machine for getting her through school by helping her tolerate the excessive stimulation of her environment.

Fortunately, we can create our own squeeze machine with our arms. It may feel silly or even simplistic, but try wrapping your arms around yourself and closing your eyes. Adding a few alternating taps on your shoulders will simply deepen your experience of serenity.

Reflection: Is it easy or challenging to give yourself a hug?

NATURAL WONDER

What: View objects of nature to ground yourself.

Stop what you are doing and bring your attention to small items from nature that you have collected in a bowl, basket, or box (shells, sea glass, acorns, pinecones, stones, feathers, leaves or the like). Look for the tiniest details. Notice the colors and textures. Conjure a moment of curiosity and wonder. Add to and change your collection when you happen upon something new. Display it visibly if you wish.

When: Between clients or whenever you're caught up in the current of the day.

Why: Have you ever noticed in autumn how the leaves float without urgency to their resting place on the ground? Or the silence as you dive beneath the surface of water, the alive stillness? We arrive in the natural world via our senses, whether it's a hike in the mountains, gardening on a Saturday, or diving beneath the waves. Through our senses, we connect with the unhurried and familiar quality of the natural world. When we bring our attention to natural forms and textures, to familiar objects that connect us to a large and peaceful world, our minds calm and bodies relax. Taking the time to examine and play with objects from nature is an exercise in mindfulness. It is an opportunity to be fully present, break the stressful spiral of your day, and slow the stream of repetitive thinking.

In his book, *Stillness Speaks*, Eckhart Tolle writes of the power of nature to bring us in to the present moment: "Look

> at a tree, a flower, a plant. Let your awareness rest upon it. How still they are, how deeply rooted in being. Allow nature to teach you stillness" (2003, p. 5).

The first time I donned a snorkel and mask, a whole new world opened to me. It was a winter break from college and my grandmother had generously taken my sister, mother, and me on a Caribbean cruise. Together, we took an outing to see tropical fish and coral reefs.

I was amazed. I had never seen such depth of beauty and vibrancy of details. The sun reflected off of parrotfish, blue corals, and seahorses. Here was a world unto itself, a world completely removed from college courses, parties, and grades.

I took home a little bit of the sea and kept a small bowl in my dorm room filled with shells, bits of sea glass, coral, and a sand dollar. Whenever I felt stressed by college life, I would 'go' to the sea. Sometimes I would line up my treasures, stack them, or just turn them over and over in my hands. As I did, I would recollect the underwater world of those Caribbean waters and let the vast sea take me beyond my own small concerns.

I once suggested a basket of natural wonders to an anxious client. The next week she described how she had experimented with a box filled with sand and shells, running her hands through it whenever she felt anxious. The tactile experience calmed her and helped her feel connected to something larger than herself.

I have kept my collection through the years, adding river stones, acorn caps, feathers, and other objects of natural beauty to my office cache. My ex-scientist husband, Daniel, will sometimes add a stone and tell me its million-year story. Whenever I get overwhelmed by the heady business of life, or notice that I've taken on the stress of too many clients, I tether myself to earth's natural beauty. I go to my baskets and bowls for imagination, connection, and grounding. There is something about touching these nature treasures that brings me to a place of stillness as I transcend my minute concerns.

Reflection: What small objects connect you to the natural world?

FINGER FOOD

What: Still yourself with a simple yogic chant.

Close your eyes and say the syllables *Sa Ta Na Ma* over and over again. While doing this, touch your fingers to your thumb on both hands simultaneously, like this:

Thumb to pointer finger—say 'Sa'
Thumb to middle finger—say 'Ta'
Thumb to ring finger—say 'Na'
Thumb to pinkie—say 'Ma'

Repeat the sequence first out loud, then in a whisper, then silently in your head.

When: If you are feeling unsettled, teary, or rattled in some way and need to calm down quickly.

Why: This mindfulness exercise combines a cognitive redirect with the calming effects of a rhythmic chant. Together, the shift of attention from unsettling thoughts to tactile experience and the slow and even recitation of simple sounds quiets the nervous system and provides an immediate sense of being anchored. A growing number of clinical experiments have demonstrated the calming and healing value of this practice, called Kirtan Kriya in Kundalini Yoga (e.g., Moss et al., 2012). The Sanskrit syllables, sa, ta, na, and ma symbolize birth, life, destruction, and regeneration, respectively. Remembering this as we say them repeatedly taps us into the cycle of all living things. The effect is profound and centering.

Despite the ethical and professional boundaries that we learn to keep, I am sometimes struck by the similarity between me and my clients. Each of us is a person on a journey, a soul doing the best we can. Sometimes it feels like the veil between *therapist* and *client* is paper thin. One late summer morning, I was reminded of the parallel human struggles I share with my clients.

It was about 8:45 a.m. on a nondescript Tuesday and I was getting ready for my 9 a.m. client, my first appointment of the day. *White noise machine on, check; air conditioner on, check; session notes reviewed, check.* My cell phone rang. It was the veterinarian's office. They weren't supposed to call until the afternoon.

My beloved dog Hickory had been at the vet's office overnight for observation and testing. He had, at age twelve, been listless at home. His appetite had decreased and he wasn't acting like himself.

The vet told me that Hickory had a giant mass in his stomach that would likely kill him within a few months. Surgery was an option but there was no guarantee. They would wait for my decision.

As I hung up, I burst into tears. *Dear old Hickory. I'm not ready for him to die* (is anyone ever ready?). I glanced at the clock. *Darn. Pull it together.* I looked up at the ceiling trying to stem the tears. *Not now*, I thought. *Think about this later. My client will be here any minute.*

In my need for immediate grounding and perspective, I remembered one of my favorite micro-self-care tools. I rested into my desk chair and recited the syllables *Sa Ta Na Ma*, while pressing my thumb to successive fingers in a pattern of serenity. As I progressed through this easy chant, I was able to bring my attention to the delicate tingle on my fingertips and the sound of my own voice. I calmed quickly and my tears stopped flowing.

I powdered my nose and entered the session room ready to be present for my client.

Her first words were, "I can't cry today because I'm going to work right after this."

Julie was a recent widow whose twenty-four-year-old son lived at home with her. As the session proceeded, Julie reported that her son, Andrew, had just been transferred by his job and would be moving out of state by month's end. As she told me about this unexpected news, she burst into tears.

"No," she said adamantly. "I cannot cry right now. I have to be composed for work."

The echo of my own *Sa Ta Na Ma* still fresh in my ears, I taught Julie this ancient technique. Together we repeated the sacred sounds, whispering the words, speaking them to the universe. Together, we postponed our tears and calmed our bodies.

By session's end, Julie felt put together enough to go out and face her workday. There would be a time for tears, a time to grieve a son's moving, and a time to grieve a dog's eminent passing. For now, there was calm.

Reflection: What self-soothing techniques do you use to calm yourself?

TURN CHEEK

What: Open a closed heart in the face of criticism.

Hold the idea in your mind that when someone presents you with anger, negativity, or criticism, they are suffering in some way. Close your eyes and breathe in the wish to take away their unhappiness. As you breathe out, imagine them receiving goodwill or comfort. This can be challenging—our instinct might be to give them an equal measure of negativity. Instead, try turning the other cheek.

When: When you receive negative or nasty feedback from a client or colleague.

Why: This technique for dealing with someone else's suffering is called tonglen in Tibetan Buddhism. It is a word that means "giving and taking." It refers to the practice of visualizing breathing in the suffering of another and sending them loving kindness with your out breath. In other words, you take their suffering and give them peace. Tonglen is a method to meet the suffering of others without resistance. It is used to generate positive emotion and non-reactivity. In Pema Chodron's bestselling book *When Things Fall Apart*, she presents tonglen as one of the three primary methods of coping with chaos. Don't allow yourself to respond to negativity with negativity—you will only be drawn into the suffering. This technique benefits both the giver and receiver.

Early in my career, I was reluctant to work with borderline personality disorder patients. I assumed I wouldn't have the stomach to withstand their displeasure, inevitable disappointment, and downright anger. But displeasure and disappointment can't be avoided. Becoming an author and a public speaker, I set myself up for judgment, anger, criticism, and displeasure.

Happily, I mostly receive positive feedback after a public presentation. Or, sometimes the criticism I receive is benignly constructive with comments such as, "wish there had been handouts" or "please repeat the questions so that the people in the back of the room can hear them." Those are easy to digest. But negative feedback, or negative book reviews for example, those always produce a slight ouch. I try not to let the opinions of others control my feelings, but it is hard not to feel happy when I am received positively and sad when received negatively. I am human.

However, there is a particular kind of negative feedback that has prompted the regular practice of this tool—an angry encounter from a bereaved parent. Bereaved parents are so devastated by their crushing loss that they are extremely skeptical of helping professionals who have not lost a child. Their negativity toward me, someone who is not a bereaved parent, can feel unkind and cutting when I feel like I'm doing my best to help.

I might hear or read a comment like, "How dare you presume to know how we feel?" or "Who do you think you are?" Rather than respond with defensiveness, I try to recognize immediately that this person is in terrible pain. I know they are suffering and feeling alone in the world with their sorrow.

I turn the mirror away from myself and toward them. Their anger is about their pain and not about me.

Recognizing their human suffering puts me in a place where I don't take their comments personally. I am then able to respond with compassion and a desire to remove their pain. Using the tonglen tool is a way to keep me feeling positive and circulate compassion. For me, this keeps my heart open and prevents the knee-jerk reaction of defensiveness.

Reflection: Are you sensitive to the comments clients, colleagues, or the public say about you? How might you feel differently if you practiced this tool?

HEAVEN AND EARTH

What: Prepare yourself for a resistant client.

Put your right hand up to the sky, pointing heavenwards. Put your left hand downwards, pointing to the ground. Feel yourself stretch up and down, simultaneously. Then switch sides with your left hand pointing up and your right hand stretching down. Speak your intentions, such as, "May I be an agent for change", "I release my expectations in order to meet the needs of my client today", or "May I be a voice between heaven and earth."

When: Before a session with a client who is highly resistant or stuck.

Why: When we encounter clients who seem resistant to change even as we watch them suffer, it is not unnatural to dig in our heels and push a little harder. Yet, there is growing literature showing that pushing for change only increases resistance. William Miller and Stephen Rollnick introduced the method of motivational interviewing, for example, which is based on the premise that a client's motivation for change grows best in an environment of acceptance and non-resistance. Miller and Rollnick write, "Resistance is an interpersonal phenomenon, and how the counselor responds will influence whether it increases or decreases" (2002, p. 40). Likewise, Judy Ringer, an Aikido master and author of *Unlikely Teachers*, reminds us that the greatest opportunity for partnership and effective change comes out of flowing with resistance rather than against it.

The openness of the pose in this practice, adapted from an exercise in Donna Eden's book, *Energy Medicine*, will help you actively and intentionally let go of your own agenda, opening yourself to the direction and pace of your client's change process. For some, looking to your higher power will be your source for acceptance and non-resistance.

Mary's husband had committed suicide. She never saw it coming. One day he told her he loved her and talked about what they would have for dinner. The next day, she found him in the garage with the car engine on.

Mary had been with her husband through his years of depression and was aware that he had started drinking a bit more than usual in recent months. She tortured herself now for not doing more: "I should have known. I should have recognized the signs and found him some help," she said.

Mary was merciless in her self-blame and her list of regrets and shortcomings. I tried everything to help her: working on her self-talk, helping her question her thoughts, engaging her in a process of self-forgiveness. I tried moving her past self-recrimination and into more grief work.

But nothing seemed to budge her from her self-punishment. It is extremely hard to keep working with someone who is making no outward progress. Of course, as therapists, we know there are rarely quick fixes in the session room. Still, we look for those subtle shifts and small measures of progress that demonstrate positive change.

Week after week, Mary sat across from me in unchanging

despair and reiterated her sense of regret. "I should have seen the signs. This shouldn't have happened."

One week, I finally let go of my expectations for change. I did the *Heaven and Earth* stretch before our session and approached our work with a posture of non-resistance and acceptance. I felt reconnected with my purpose and my higher power. The power to change was out of my hands.

I asked Mary if she felt therapy was helping her and commented that she still seemed quite entrenched in her feelings of regret and self-recrimination. She nodded, and confirmed it was true that she still felt crippled by regret. And yet, she said she derived comfort from being with me. "I would be so much worse off if I wasn't able to come here." I was dumbstruck.

Even when a client appears stuck or isn't making progress toward the goals in our treatment plans, our non-judgmental presence is still helping more than we know. I find that using this "heaven and earth" practice before a seemingly 'stuck' client helps me release tension and preconceived expectations for change. Remembering my higher power makes me feel backed up by the Universe. I try to abide in the knowledge that my presence is supportive and that I am a conduit for a healing energy.

Reflection: What words or phrases help you remember to be more patient with a 'resistant' client.

HELLO KITTY

What: Surround yourself with self-compassion.

Place your hand tenderly on your cheek. Say to yourself, "May I be at ease. May I accept myself. May I know deep peace. May I be kind to myself." You can use any gentle, supportive, loving words that resonate for you.

When: Try this every day before your first client. Also use when you are feeling overwhelmed or self-critical.

Why: A gentle attitude toward oneself is the basis for self-care. If we look to Buddhism, we see that the first stage in the metta bhavana, the loving-kindness meditation exercise prescribed by the Buddha himself, is to offer loving-kindness to oneself. In Buddhism, it is believed that one cannot offer love to another until she has learned to love ourselves.

Kristin Neff is an expert and leading clinical researcher on self-compassion. In her book *Self Compassion: The Proven Power of Being Kind to Yourself*, she emphasizes that self-compassion not only tames our depressing and sometimes debilitating self-criticism but creates a heightened self-clarity and nourishing environment for inner healing and growth.

Lack of self-esteem and the propensity for self-blame are at the heart of many of our clients' challenges. As we accompany our clients on their journey toward a more gentle and loving attitude toward themselves, so must we be able to model that attitude.

Rosie had come to see me because she was confused about her life. At twenty-three years old, she had just broken up with a boyfriend who had been verbally abusive. She didn't have much self-direction and felt stalled in her work as a waitress in a pizza restaurant. She had also recently terminated a pregnancy and felt enormous guilt over her decision.

"I don't regret what I did," she said, "not exactly. I mean, I know that raising a child by myself would have been a nightmare. And Bruce would have been a terrible dad, like the *worst*."

As she spun out her tale of guilt, grief, and confusion, she said, "I guess I've turned out exactly like my mom said I would. I'm a fuck-up." Her eyes filled with tears.

"Oh sweetheart," I said (mimicking the words of the teacher, Byron Katie, author of *Loving What Is*). "You are so hard on yourself." She nodded, holding in tears.

"Have you always been so hard on yourself?" I prodded. She nodded her head *yes*.

I responded slowly and quietly, "Would you like to learn some ways to be gentle with yourself."

"I don't know how to do that," she said, blowing her nose.

I knew she was describing a common experience for many people, young and old, blue and white collar, doctors and high school dropouts, clients and therapists. We don't know how to be compassionate with ourselves.

In contrast, we do know how to criticize, judge, and blame ourselves. We're experts at self-violence. Ask us to switch from self-violence to self-compassion and we often haven't the slightest idea.

I asked Rosie if she would be willing to do a visualization exercise with me. Upon her agreement, we embarked together on a simple journey.

"Picture yourself sitting in a sunny meadow. Put your hand on your cheek and say, *Oh you sweet thing, you dear one.*"

Rosie said this mechanically, with no emotion.

"Okay," I said "Next, imagine that you see a little kitten in the rain. Walk up to the kitten, lean down to it, and say, *Oh you sweet little thing, you dear one.*"

This time Rosie said the words with emotion and emphasis.

"Now, I want you to take that deep emotion, the heartfelt feeling that you have for the little wet kitten and direct it toward yourself. Imagine your little self drenched in the rain and try to feel that same tenderness toward yourself. Say, *Oh you sweet thing, you dear one.*"

She tried again and tears came to her eyes. Although her tone wasn't quite a sweet as it had been toward the kitten, it was definitely an improvement over her first attempt.

Rosie said she was willing to try to be gentler with herself and use this technique to increase her capacity for self-love. When we love something, we take care of it.

Reflection: How does your day go differently when you send yourself loving kindness in the morning?

GO WITH THE FLOW

What: Stop the spiral of repetitive thinking or stressful thoughts.

Let the bathroom be a place for a brief respite. As you wash your hands, direct your attention to the feel of the water, its temperature and fluidity. Focus on the force of the water, the gurgling sounds it makes as it falls from your hands and makes its way down the drain. Let the water cue you to reset yourself and, just for this moment, let your thoughts and worries wash down the drain. If lotion is something you use, continue this mindful moment as you apply it to your hands. Pay attention to its tactile quality, the sensations on your fingers, and the aroma.

When: Between clients.

Why: This tool, first published in my earlier book, *Shortcuts to Inner Peace*, is a mindfulness practice of nonjudgmental, present awareness. It means being completely awake to your experience as opposed to going through the motions on autopilot. Not only will allowing yourself a moment of awareness give you the opportunity to check in with your inner feeling states, it will set you up for a higher level of awareness as you enter your next client session. Mindful awareness practices are the building blocks for developing what Dan Siegel has termed "mindsight." In his book, *The Mindful Therapist*, he writes, "Rather than being consumed by worries about the future or pre-occupations with the past, living in the present is an art form that liberates the mind to relieve

> mental suffering. These are the ways we develop presence in our own lives. Being present can also be seen as the most important element of helping others heal" (2010, p. 1).

"I really prefer to have gaps between clients," said my friend and colleague Karen Horneffer-Ginter, a therapist in Michigan and author of the book, *Full Cup, Thirsty Spirit*. Karen and I were discussing self-care practices.

She continued, "But some days, I have to just stack those clients up, one after the other, maybe even four in a row. Some days it just can't be helped."

"I know," I commiserated. "Do you do anything differently on those days, with regards to keeping yourself paced for the marathon?"

She chuckled, "I wash my hands." We both giggled—as if she didn't wash her hands on other days.

She continued, "I wash my hands very intentionally. Clients think I'm just going to the bathroom between sessions. What they don't know is that I'm engaging in a hand washing ritual that makes it possible for me to come back into the room."

Karen began to describe all the ways water brings her back to herself. She feels the water and lets a cascade of thoughts and images flow: third world countries in which women have to walk to rivers or wells for their water, country dwellers who lose their water with every power outage, and the ubiquity of water in lakes, oceans, waterfalls, and rivers all around the world.

Our own bodies are approximately two-thirds water. Water is our life force. We are drawn to water. For Karen, she is calmed and filled with gratitude, using her moment with the faucet to redirect her thoughts and focus her attention. For others, the simple exercise of mindful awareness enlivens their sense of wellbeing and readies them to continue the day with greater clarity.

As I listened to Karen talk about the positive effects of mindfully washing her hands between clients, I was reminded of a similar intentional experience with lotion. When I first moved to New Hampshire I shared an office suite with several other psychotherapists. One of the other therapists put a lotion in the bathroom called "Kiss My Face." It was a luxury item, a Chinese honey and oleander flower fragrance that is no longer available. (I know because I've looked.)

This particular variety of lotion was so deliciously exotic that I would sometimes linger in the bathroom massaging it on my hands with sheer delight. Just those few moments of lotion magic made me feel as if I was on a mini-vacation. For me, this mindful experience prompted feelings of rejuvenation and joy.

Reflection: Which mindfulness habit serves you best?

ANCHORS AWAY

What: Make your work environment a place that nourishes you.

Have at least one item that you can view from your chair that anchors you to a calm feeling. Let it be an anchor for your pleasant emotions, a visible reminder to help you return to rootedness. When you find your anchor object, practice focusing on the associated pleasant sensations.

When: During sessions, when you are feeling vulnerable to your client's story and emotions, or when you notice in yourself increasing arousal or reactivity.

Why: Because we respond well to visual cues, this tool quickly reduces hyperarousal. Similar to Rothschild's concept of sensory anchor, an object associated with happy memories triggers feelings associated with a safe place (2006, p. 120). By placing an item in your office that acts as a visual anchor to your inner sanctuary, you can go to it when you wish to calm your body and mind.

"I think of my office space as my co-therapist," said a colleague of mine. "Every single item in my office is there for a reason." Like a poem where every word matters, her room was filled with treasures with a purpose. For her, everything from the wall color to the furniture to the special objects placed around the room told a story.

"Everything about my work is geared to creating emotional safety for my clients, so my room has to do the same," she said. "And it isn't just for my clients. I need to feel the safety, too."

When I was a social work student, I had an internship in a large community mental health center. There were many employees and students all vying for coveted office space. I often moved from office to office to see clients. I carried a small tote of client charts, a vagabond roving the halls. Some days I was able to settle into one office, but others, each client meant a new room.

One day I was mildly complaining to my supervisor about how unsettling it was to move from office to office, never knowing exactly where I'd be. I was also miffed that not every office had a clock in it, making it awkward for me as I tried to inconspicuously look at my wristwatch to determine if time was up.

My supervisor sympathized with my unfortunate circumstance. She suggested I have my own clock that I bring from place to place. She also suggested I bring an anchor item to each office, something that would personalize the space for me.

I knew she couldn't mean a personal photograph since that sort of self-disclosure wasn't encouraged. "Something you find beautiful or calming," she suggested.

I thought about it and happened upon a shell, a gorgeous shell that reminded me of the calm and bliss I experience at my favorite beach. Just looking at it made me feel centered and happy. I took that simple shell from room to room and found that it truly had an anchoring effect.

Now, happily, I have a gorgeous home office that is filled to bursting with objects that I find lovely, calming, and sustaining. It is a sanctuary for me. And on the table next to where my clients sit, a table that holds tissues, a coaster, my business cards, and a pen, I still have that beautiful shell.

Reflection: When you look at your anchor during session, how does it make you feel?

PHOTO SHOP

What: Restore a feeling of love and human connection.

Look at a photograph of a beloved person or pet. Recollect or imagine the moment of the photograph—the mood, feelings, setting. Allow yourself to smile at your loved one. Keep a photo in your desk drawer or have a selection of photos on your phone, computer, or in your wallet.

When: When you have a short break between sessions.

Why: In the midst of a busy day, feeling tired and rushed, it is easy to lose your sense of compassion, your appreciation of human connections. Memories and images of people or animals you love will trigger feelings of attachment, relationship, and contact, recreating that sense of engagement with your loved one. Opening your heart will allow you to enter the space of therapy with greater calm, less judgment, and more accurate empathy.

For two years, he was my co-therapist. He wasn't licensed or even trained. He didn't even have a degree. But my faithful furry companion, Hickory, had, at times, perhaps a greater therapeutic impact on my clients than I did. He certainly had a profound impact on me.

When Hickory, a handsome golden retriever, was twelve years old, he was given a terminal diagnosis. As I wrote previously (Finger Food), Hickory had a large internal mass that was likely cancerous. We elected he have surgery to remove the mass, knowing there was no guarantee that this procedure would prolong his life. Fortunately, it bought us three more years with Hickory.

In those ensuing years, Hickory and I became inseparable. Even though I have a home office, he had never before had the patience to sit in on my sessions. Now he seemed eager to rest at my feet while I worked with my clients. Although he still sometimes exhibited a burst of puppy-like enthusiasm, he grew more infirm by the day. He could no longer walk up and down stairs and he frequently slipped. Hardwood floors caused him to splay out like Bambi on ice.

Always a gentle soul, Hickory became even sweeter as he aged. My clients adored him. The depressed man smiled. The recalcitrant teen got on the floor and buried her face in his fur. The curmudgeonly crone crooned to him. The bitter couple fussed together over him. Everyone loved Hickory.

Between sessions, I would get down on the floor and love on Hickory. I'd scratch his tummy and kiss his adorable face and he would reward me with adoration.

Three years passed. He became diminished, nearly blind, virtually deaf, bony and frail. But his spirit was strong and loving. A month before his fifteenth birthday, he crossed the Rainbow Bridge, a place, they say, where deceased pets wait for their masters. My clients and I mourned him. The teenager cried with me.

Now, between clients, I look at a photograph of Hickory and allow that deep and vast unconditional love to imprint itself on my heart. I use the time between sessions to shore up my storehouse of love.

I enjoy looking at photographs of my husband and children as well. But I have to confess that my favorite *photo shop* experience is when I reflect on Hickory. His absence is noted in the therapy room, but his love fills my heart just the same.

Reflection: Does your day feel different when you intentionally fill your heart with love between sessions?

ROOTS

What: Reinvigorate your body and clarify your self-awareness.

Stand tall and imagine you are a tree. Close your eyes and feel yourself rooted to the earth. Let your feelings, sensations, and emotions rise up as you imagine the earth's nutrients rising through your feet and up into your body. Feel your trunk resonate with energy. Now lift your arms upward, as if they are swaying branches and imagine the sun's energy joining you to the sky above, connecting you in a vertical pillar of energy. Trees are graceful images of change, strength, transformation, and regeneration. Be a tree.

When: At the end of your day, especially if your energy is flagging.

Why: For millennia in the yogic traditions, aligning the spine and head has been known to be an openhearted posture, one that allows for both wakefulness and calm. The roots practice is a modified version of the traditional Yoga tree pose that energizes, rebalances, and provides a good stretch. In modern Buddhism the great Zen master, Shunryu Suzuki, writes that in meditation, the straight spine allows one to keep mental and physical balance (1970). Using rich metaphors such as the tree to inspire us is one way of expanding our sense of possibility and connectedness to the natural world.

If you're like me, you get a lot of emails. I am on so many email lists that I sometimes feel lost under the barrage of constant incoming communications. Often I hit delete before I open the message.

Last year, I received emails from an organization called the Lightworker's Healing Method regarding a training series. They offered four levels of training in energetic healing work. It caught my attention, but not enough to compel me to sign up. At the time, it struck me as perhaps a bit too 'woo-woo.'

One day I received an email regarding a special promotion. They were holding a drawing for a free pass to an upcoming level one class and all you had to do was sign up with your name and email. For me, it seemed like a low risk way to possibly win a free training. Guess what? I won. And just like that, I found myself listening to ten hours of training with Lynn McGonagill, author of *The Lightworkers Healing Method*.

I found myself impressed with Lynn's infectious enthusiasm and uplifted energy. She taught about energy work, self-care, being guided and supported in our important work—and she taught about earth energy. She insisted, in fact, that we need to draw up earth energy from the center of the earth and into our own bodies. In doing this, she promised, we will be grounded and strong.

I found myself imagining a tall tree as she spoke. She described a pillar of vertical energy that I saw embodied as a tree. I think the life of a tree is the perfect example of graceful change, and its form a natural symbol for calm presence and upright living. Whether you prefer the imagery of earth energy, the balancing quality of the tree pose, or simply need a good stretch, place your feet firmly on the floor and reach for the sky.

Reflection: Can you see a tree from your office?

GOOD FOR ME

What: Acknowledge work well done.

Put your hand over your heart and pat your chest as you say the words, "Good for me." Say this phrase three times in a row while patting your chest.

When: After you have a planned final session with a client, or a single successful encounter with someone you're not likely to see again.

Why: It's important to honor endings and acknowledge your good work. I learned this self-care tool from Alaya Chadwick, author of *Wake up to Your (W)hole Life*. She advises using it liberally. As helpers, we encounter many challenges through our week. The wrong turns, false starts, botched endings, miscalculations, and misadventures stay with us despite our best efforts. This self-care tool is designed to give our successes a fighting chance. Honor your happy endings and completed successes with a ritual that uses the good in your life to boost your self-confidence and mood and honors the positive connections that transpired between you and your clients.

When I was an intern at a family counseling center, I worked with a family of whom I was especially fond. The family consisted of a mom, dad, and two daughters, ages twelve and ten. The parents were getting divorced and they wanted to have a few sessions together to talk about the impact of the divorce on the children and how they could make it as smooth a process as possible.

I was impressed. The late 1980's weren't exactly the dark ages of divorce, but it was still refreshing to work with a couple ready to embark on a collaborative, peaceful process. Of course, the sessions weren't always quite so peaceful. Painful issues were revisited, reasons why they felt so incompatible. I tried to keep the sessions focused on the kids and what would be best for them. I also had my own countertransference to stay aware of because the older daughter, April, reminded me so much of myself. I, too, had been twelve years old when my parents decided to separate and then divorce.

April was tearful during the family sessions but also insightful about the changes that were being forced on her. During one session, April became so angry that she ran out of the room. I remember being completely bewildered and at a loss. The father looked at me and asked, "Should I go get her?" Just as I was resisting the urge to shrug and say, "Don't ask me, I'm just a student," the daughter returned on her own volition.

Our sixth session was a planned termination. I have to say that I love planned terminations because they feel more the exception than the norm. Many clients, I think, find it too hard to say goodbye so they never quite make that last session. Others drift out of treatment before their work is completed. Therefore, a planned and well-executed ending is a treat—a chance to review our work together, reflect on growth, let them know the door is always open, and say goodbye.

With this family, we hugged at the end of our final session and April teared up as she thanked me. I was deeply moved. After the session was over, I sat in my chair and had no idea what to do. I wanted to cry but felt that I couldn't. In fact, I didn't want to feel whatever it was that I was feeling. I called a friend. I didn't tell her that I had just had a profound final session but couldn't sit with my own feelings. Instead we chatted aimlessly for awhile. I felt nauseated for the rest of the night.

I could have talked with my supervisor, but what I really needed was to sit with my feelings and honor the work I had done with this family. I was sad to say goodbye and happy that I had known them. *Good for me* for being able to be present with a family during a critical time in their lives. *Good for me* for trying my best to be helpful even when I didn't always know what to do. *Good for me* for opening myself honoring to them and gifting them with my presence. *Good for me* for their courage in facing a tremendous challenge.

Endings are perfect times to take stock and remember that our work is meaningful, and ultimately sacred.

Reflection: Can you notice, accept, and honor the impact you have on other people's lives?

EMPTY CUP

What: Put yourself in a relaxed state of clear thinking and receptivity.

Sit in your chair and cup your hands together, creating a small 'cup'. Close your eyes and notice the inner sensations of your hands as they form the empty cup. Bring your complete attention to this inner body awareness and witness the sensations as they arise.

When: When you are expecting a session of heightened emotion, or you find yourself distracted before an important session. Do this practice right before the session begins.

Why: It is important to remain aware (before, during, and after a session) of our internal responses to our clients' stories. When you focus your attention on your inner body you experience interoception, an internal sense of visceral body sensations. Interoception allows you to watch your own somatic emotional reactions. Eckhart Tolle talks about the grounding effects of tracking your inner body. He suggests closing your eyes and noticing how you still 'know' that your hands are there, even when you don't see them. You sense them. Practicing interoception before a session brings you out of distracted thinking and creates a heightened level of dual awareness that leads to effective therapy.

Though the session ahead is uncertain, know that you don't need to resist; just witness and accept. Called mudras, in Sanskrit, hand gestures are commonly used in the yogic tradition to facilitate the flow of energy through the body. With cupped hands, you create a symbolic space of receptivity and openness.

I would say that most of the time, I have no idea what is going to happen in a session. I typically reread my previous session notes to remind myself what we last discussed and whether I assigned any homework. But often, I don't have a specific direction that I plan to take. I might have only a vague impression at best of what might come up or what direction we'll be moving in.

Janice was a fifty-two-year-old woman whose twenty-seven-year-old daughter, Brittany, had succumbed to a heroin addiction. Janice had stood by her daughter's side during a ten-year battle that included enabling, tough love, twelve steps, four rehab stints, and countless relapses. Janice had given up on Brittany quite a few times only to turn around in this agonizing dance and try again. The dance ended when Brittany overdosed and was found in her apartment by a neighbor.

In this session, Janice reported she was nervous about picking up Brittany's ashes because she didn't think she could handle it. Still, she was determined to spread the ashes in a place she had visited with Brittney on the slopes of Mount Washington called The Lake in the Clouds. Their annual trips to this special place recalled a happy time, long before the divorce, long before the addiction. Janice was afraid she would have a panic attack on the mountain and had convinced a friend to accompany her.

The morning of my next appointment with Janice was filled with picayune business details that had doused my present moment awareness and left me swamped by a heady to-do list: scheduling a CEU workshop, rearranging sessions, emailing a potential client, and filling out a malpractice insurance renewal form. I was five minutes from talking with a woman about her sacred journey to spread her daughter's ashes and didn't want to be thinking about whether my credit card had expired. I needed to bring myself into my body, this room, and a place of nonresistance and receptivity.

The simple practice of noticing my inner body helped me to regain awareness of my present state and purpose. It allowed for a dramatic shift in perspective from that of stressed office worker to helper, administrator to holder of the sacred. I took off my many hats and moved back into the role of therapist.

As it turns out, the experience was everything that Janice had expected and more. The climb was arduous; she did have a panic attack; she did sob when she spread the ashes; and . . . she was moved beyond words by the power evoked by such an awesome task. While on the mountain, she was flooded with beautiful memories of Brittany's precious soul. She even felt her daughter's presence all around her.

Janice told me, "In the eyes of society, Brittany was just an addict. But I know she was so much more than that."

I leaned forward, fully present and engaged, and commented, "Don't ever let your daughter be defined by her illness and death. Let her be defined by the brightness of her life and the love that you will always carry in your heart."

We both smiled.

Reflection: What domestic chores or between session tasks keep you from being prepared for your sacred work?

REPEAT AFTER ME

What: Ground yourself against reactivity with a calming mantra.

This micro-self-care practice offers a technique for vigilantly monitoring your emotional reactions. Find a phrase that resonates with you such as: "Patience, patience, patience," "Everything is as it should be," "I'm grateful for this opportunity to notice my own reactivity," or "I will not give my power away." Or repeat a single word that is meaningful for you, such as "peace" or "serenity." When you notice yourself feeling reactive, repeat your phrase or word and respond out of awareness.

When: When you find yourself frustrated, triggered, fearful, or activated in some manner by a client or colleague. Perhaps you've waited on the phone with an insurance company for twenty minutes, had a client storm out of your office, learned that funding for the addiction groups just got cut, or been chastised by your supervisor.

Why: We pride ourselves on our ability to ride that fine boundary between accurate empathy and emotional involvement. Yet sometimes, in or out of session, we may find ourselves in situations that test our ability to stay cool. In those most heated or frustrating situations, when we feel our amygdala heat up and our prefrontal cortex go offline, it takes a high degree of self-awareness and practiced restraint to calm our reactivity. In speaking or thinking a mantra, we calm our reactivity by redirecting our attention to the calming effect of a rhythmic chant. In the Christian tradition, repetitive centering prayer has the same effect. This repeat after me self-care practice helps us maintain equanimity.

Your self-talk not only reflects your state of being but also guides it. Thus, watch and choose the words you say to reflect how you want to be in the world.

My amygdala took over the day my eighteen-year-old client, who had been treated for a dual diagnosis even before her father died (of alcohol dependence and clinical depression) told me she had a *gun in her purse.*

I felt my heart simultaneously race and seemingly stop. "A gun in your purse?" I said with alarm, all therapeutic neutrality lost.

She said casually, "Well, it's not like it's loaded or anything."

"Jenny," I said quietly, "Why do you have an unloaded gun in your purse?"

She got teary-eyed, "I want you to take it . . . I'm afraid that I'm going to use it to kill myself."

"Oh honey . . ." I remarked.

With that, she began sobbing uncontrollably. In between sobs, she told me she had been thinking of hurting herself and that she just wanted to go be with her dad. Her wish was to die.

It's not unusual for grievers to want to leave the planet and reunite with their loved one. However, a young griever with a plan, means of intent, and a history of depression and alcohol dependence—that's a complicated wish.

Thoughts began to swirl in my head. *I need to hospitalize this girl. I don't have the time to take her to the hospital. I've never done this before. Oh my God! A gun!*

Realizing that my fight or flight instinct had been activated, in a last ditch effort to avert panic I offered myself positive affirmations. *I can do this. All is well.* And as a friend of mine says, "*There is a way; there is always a way, and the way is on the way.*"

After listening to Jenny for some time, I took her gun and left the room. I called a colleague on my supervision team for quick feedback on my decision, cancelled my next appointment, spoke with Jenny's emergency contact, and called the hospital.

In the end, Jenny rode with her mother to the hospital and I followed, chanting my mantras the whole way. She checked in with psychiatric admissions and I turned the gun over to the admitting nurse.

As I left Jenny, I hugged her and said, "Repeat after me: *I'm going to be ok. All is well.*" Even as she walked away from me, she was repeating, "I'm going to be OK."

And she was.

Reflection: What words bring you solace that bear repeating?

WHITE LIGHT

What: Visualize a protective barrier around your body.

Imagine a wide beam of white light coming down from the ceiling and spotlighting you in its rays. See yourself completely encased in the light, as it surrounds and protects you, like a cocoon.

When: In a session (or afterwards) when you feel you are reacting to or mirroring a client you perceive as caustic, negative, hostile, hopeless, or depressed. Also, if you are feeling attacked by a client in some way.

Why: We are potentially like sponges, at risk of soaking up the emotions and feelings of the people across from us. Sometimes the cause is counter-transference, when our past experiences are awakened by our clients' responses to us. Other times, it is simply our nervous system's evolved empathic response, a result of our ability to tune in to another's emotions and respond with the same feelings. Rothschild describes our unconscious tendency to respond in kind to our clients' emotions when we unconsciously mimic their body posture and facial expressions (2006). Other times, clients might simply be threatening. This white light practice uses the imagery of a protective shield to elevate and maintain awareness of your separate body and emotions.

Sometimes we offer the only place where a client can express a feeling or tell a story. I have had many grievers tell me, upon crying in my office, that they haven't been able to cry anywhere else. In their outside lives, they are so distracted and defensive that they stay at arm's length from their feelings. Coming into the quiet sanctuary of the therapy room with no other purpose but to feel and reflect, their tears readily rise to the surface.

For me, holding tears feels like an easy job. However, I have also had clients tell me that they come to me to dump all of their feelings. One such client told me that the therapy room was a perfect dumping ground for her anger and her resentment. She had been cheated on by not one but two men. Trust was now a big issue for her, particularly in situations where she felt vulnerable. In my experience, holding grievances is a much harder job than holding sorrow.

The first time she dumped her feelings on me, I felt absolutely exhausted at the end of the session. In fact, as we wrapped up our time together, she exclaimed, "I feel so much better! I feel ten pounds lighter. It helps me so much to get this venom off my chest." She bounced out of the office while I practically fell to the ground behind her, weighed down by the heavy emotions that I had mirrored and internalized.

I had a pounding headache and felt ill for almost thirty minutes. Her words echoed in my head: "Men suck. They are the lowest life form on the planet. You can never trust a man or any of his false words. The world would be an infinitely better place without men. They should be wiped out, eradicated." These were not my beliefs and hers was not my experience but I felt the emotions as if they were. Week after week she came in to rant about "despicable" men.

In discussions with my supervisory group, it became clear that this wasn't an issue of past experience for me but rather that my body was responding in kind to my client's physical and verbal expressions. I had unconsciously fallen into a pattern of somatic empathy with this client.

I entered my next session with the awareness that I needed to maintain a more intentional feeling of separation from her: *I am not my client and she is not me.* I imagined a white light as a gentle barrier wrapping me in a protective cushion, keeping me safely in the position as helper.

Feeling less assaulted, I was able to honor her feelings while maintaining a healthy separation between her emotional expression and my response. From this place of calm, I was able to guide her, slowly, to a place under her anger to where her deepest pain lay. The fear, helplessness, and guilt of her multiple betrayals were searing.

I don't know if she'll take the risk to be in a heterosexual relationship again, but to date, she has a new male friend at work whom she enjoys chatting with over lunch. She grudgingly admitted one day, "Well, maybe *all* men aren't rats."

From my column of white light, I smiled.

Reflection: What price do you pay when you mirror and absorb your clients' negative emotions?

CENTERED

What: Ready yourself for a new client with centeredness.

Focus your attention on the center of your body. Imagine this spot, located just below your navel, as secure and weighted. Just for a moment, close your eyes, breathe deeply, and, as you exhale, visualize that center of gravity connecting you firmly to this earth.

When: Before an intake session

Why: Intentionally keeping yourself feeling grounded and secure in your own body allows you to be a rock, firm in your ability to help as a new client comes into your space. Feeling rooted helps you prepare for the unexpected even as it calms the new client with the impression of openhearted confidence. This technique of tuning to your center of gravity I learned from Judy Ringer. Judy, an Aikido master and author of the book, *Unlikely Teachers*, applies the center of gravity concept to facing attackers, potential conflict, and performance anxiety. No matter what the situation, the prescription is always the same: center yourself first and everything else will flow more easily.

Marge was late. This, in and of itself, wasn't concerning because many intake clients tend to be either very early or very late. Few of my clients get lost these days now that GPS systems are routinely available.

Marge was an older woman, however, and had told me ahead of time that she didn't have one of those "newfangled" systems. I emailed her directions ahead of time but the attachment proved too difficult for her to open and so I had to send them separately via snail mail.

Preparing for an intake requires a certain amount of energy. There is the initial phone screening and preparation of a new file (both physical and electronic). There is the anticipation as you wait to see if they'll actually show up, and if so, how close to the scheduled time. And of course, there is the actual session (should it finally happen) in which you encounter the life story and current circumstances of an entirely new person.

Still, however anxiety provoking it might be for the therapist, this anticipation pales in comparison to the experience of many clients. They are frequently already in some state of crisis: they are coming to a place they've never been before, meeting a complete stranger, launching into extremely private territory, and are perhaps completely uncertain about their future.

When Marge was late, I had a hunch that she might be lost. From our initial phone conversation, I already knew she was lost in many ways. She was anxious about being alone in the world after the recent death of her husband. My heart began to beat a bit more quickly as I watched out the window toward my driveway. After about fifteen minutes, she finally called to say that she was hopelessly lost. Fortunately, it turned out she was only a few streets away.

As I waited for Marge, I took a moment to center and ground myself. When Marge arrived, she was visibly frustrated and disoriented. From my place of feeling centered, I was able to receive her calmly. I welcomed her and tried my best to put her at ease. I suggested we take a deep breath together before we began. My first question to a client is usually not "What brings you here today?" (we get to that later), but "How did you feel about coming here today?" This gives them an opportunity to express their anxiety, fear, or dread—whatever it is they're carrying into the room.

Whatever they share, I tune into my centered self and find that it's one of the best places from which to build rapport and a therapeutic alliance.

Reflection: If you don't take the time to center yourself before a first session, how does it effect your rapport with a new client?

I SURRENDER

What: Symbolically let go of your need to see your clients progress.

Remember that the direction and rate of change for clients is up to them, not you. Have a lidded basket or surrender jar for the purpose of symbolically surrendering your clients' change processes. Write on a piece of paper your client's initials. Then ball it up, and release the paper into the jar saying, "I surrender this person to their highest growth and good."

When: After or before seeing a client who you find challenging, upsetting, or difficult.

Why: This tool is an exercise in detachment from your clients' outcomes, and a practice to remember that when we, as helpers, feel upset or challenged, the therapeutic process has shifted its focus from the client to the therapist. It helps to physically and ritualistically let go of your perception of control over your clients and their destinies. You cannot control their agendas, their progress, or their outcomes. Practice in detachment from control will improve your therapeutic relationships and help you achieve a richer feeling of inner peace. Furthermore, placing paper in a jar serves as a symbolic containment exercise.

I love working with couples—I really do—but many arrive on my doorstep too late. They show up in advanced stages of distress, the equivalent of stage four cancer, if you will. And there are some relationships, sadly, that seem dead on arrival.

Fortunately for me, I am not a marriage preservationist. While I do see many couples deeply in love who strive successfully to preserve their marriage vows, I've seen others who, it turns out, got married for all of the wrong reasons. With cases of entrenched dysfunction, conflict, and years of unhappiness, ending the marriage can be the kindest outcome for everyone.

But ultimately, it isn't for me to determine who should stay together and who shouldn't. I try to guide couples to greater clarity and help them come to their own conclusions. Regardless of what's unfolding, I know that they each have their path of suffering and growth. The reason they are a couple is still unfolding and whether they continue to move forward together is yet to be seen. I believe that all struggles are part of a greater growth opportunity.

Jessie and Bob had been married for only four years when they came to see me. Bob desperately wanted the relationship to work but Jessie seemed ambivalent (even though she claimed to want to save the marriage). On his separate intake form, Bob answered the question "What would you like out of therapy?" with a clear "to save my marriage." Jessie, on the other hand, answered that same question with "to decide whether I want to stay in the marriage."

I didn't point out this difference but Bob sensed Jessie's ambivalence. He complained that she didn't want to have sex anymore. She complained that she didn't feel desire for him anymore. He complained that she didn't seem to enjoy time with him anymore. She complained that all he ever did was complain.

Both Bob and Jessie had a desperate look that pleaded, "Please fix this situation and fast." Bob asked for homework to improve their connection. Jessie asked for suggestions on how she could ignite the spark again. At times I wished that I could wave my magic wand and produce the results they desired. But ultimately, I knew that I couldn't force their progress. Nor could I make Jessie fall back in love with Bob.

Sometimes before a session with Jessie and Bob, and sometimes after, I would write out a phrase of letting go and release their outcome to my "I Surrender" jar. It helped me drop my attachment to my agenda and contain feelings of helplessness.

After months of confusion and discernment, Jessie finally decided to leave Bob. Our work gradually shifted to helping them work out an amicable separation and eventual divorce. Each of them grew into a deeper understanding of themselves and their participation in the relationship. If I had needed them to save their marriage, this conclusion would have felt like a failure to me. By surrendering their outcome I was able to see my role as counselor as critical on their unique path to greater clarity.

Reflection: What is it like for you to let go of your clients' outcomes and stick to your role as a catalyst?

ABC

What: Stop the spiral of stress with a brief meditation.

Reset your mind and body. Take three minutes of focused stillness. Only three. In these three minutes, with your eyes closed, let the following one-minute prompts be your guide: A—awareness; B—breath; C—core. In the first minute, become aware, with curiosity, of the sounds around you, the sensation of the air on your skin, and/or the pressure of your feet on the floor. In the second minute, bring your attention to your breath. Notice on your in-breath the feeling of the cool air against your nostrils and the feeling of your expanding lungs before the air returns warm against your upper lip. In the third minute, even as your breath continues naturally, let your awareness come to the core central axis of your body, like the core of an apple. Just notice. Whenever you find yourself distracted during any of the stages, just bring your attention back to the A, B, or C. To keep time, use a traditional or digital meditation timer.

When: At night, before bed.

Why: By the end of a stressful day, the non-stop chatter of our verbal left-brain is often going full tilt. Mindful awareness activates the visual-spatial right hemisphere of the brain, thus calming the day's noise. In *The Buddha's Brain*, Hanson addresses the brain mechanism called "reciprocal inhibition" which suppresses one part of the brain when another is activated. When we engage in activities like visualization and whole body awareness that activate the brain's right hemisphere, the verbal functions of the left hemisphere go offline. With practice, you will find this easy meditation can quickly calm your mind and body.

Like many of you, I have been to a lot of CEU workshops. In fact, at twenty hours of CEUs per year for twenty-five years, I've put in over five hundred hours of post-graduate training from CEU classes alone. And, of course, I've accumulated a stack of workbooks, handouts, and notes that I have always meant to revisit . . . one day. Unfortunately that day never seems to come and much of what I learned in those single days has been forgotten.

But there is one technique that has stayed with me. About ten years ago, I took a CEU class with David Treadway, author of *Intimacy, Change, and Other Therapeutic Mysteries*. Although he often lectures about couples work, this particular workshop was on spirituality. What stood out for me was his presentation of a three-minute exercise that he called "the egg timer" meditation.

Why did I find this noteworthy? Up until that point, I had always been advised to meditate for a minimum of twenty minutes. Yet, even now, I find it extremely difficult to do a long meditation. For me, with regards to meditation, less has always been more.

Many years after David's egg timer exercise, I got further validation for the idea of a short meditation from Martin Boroson's book, *One Moment Meditation*. In fact, according to Martin, I only needed one minute.

I have been using my own three-minute version for myself and with clients for some time with great success. I like to think of it as a one-minute meditation with a one-minute introduction and a one-minute closing. It's as easy as ABC. Using this practice at the end of the day helps you transition to the night before you.

Reflection: What keeps you from not doing an ABC meditation each and every evening?

WALK LIKE A MONK

What: End your day with balance and groundedness.

Walk slowly, very slowly, for three steps. Let each foot come to the ground with intention: heel, ball, toe, heel, ball, toe. Notice the pressure shifting under your feet and the texture and firmness of the floor. Pause and lift one leg to find your equilibrium. Spend a few moments in singular balance and think or say, "I am in the now. This day has come and gone. I only have now. "

When: At night before you go to sleep. This brief mindfulness practice can be performed to find balance and groundedness during any walking transition, even from one room to another.

Why: As therapists we are forever working to balance myriad details in our lives—personal with professional goals; client with office needs; needs of the self with those of our colleagues and our loved ones. For each of us, our point of balance is found in the present moment. When we practice mindful awareness of each step, we practice resting at the fulcrum. At night, we also rest in the radical acceptance that the day is over and what is done is done. The Zen Buddhist, Thich Nhat Hanh (2011, p. 8) writes:

> When you take a step, you can touch the earth in such a way that you establish yourself in the present moment. You arrive in the here and the now. You don't need to make any effort at all. Suddenly, you are free—from all projects, all worries, and all expectations.

"How about I bring Chinese food next week and we have lunch. You said you don't see clients on Fridays, so how about it?" Mariah, my sweet, sixteen-year-old client, wanted desperately to be my friend. This was our last session together because school was out and she was leaving soon to spend the summer at her grandmother's house. Mariah's father and brother had been killed in a car accident just four months ago.

I hate having to explain to a client why I cannot be their friend, have lunch, or go out for coffee, especially when I think they will not take the news easily.

Mariah insisted, "But I just don't get it. If I'm not your client anymore, why can't we have lunch? Fine. If not in your office, how about a restaurant? Please?"

Oy. There are so many balancing acts every day. Set a boundary here, make a decision there. Do I accept the handmade Christmas gift? Do I offer the hug she's asked for? Do I tell him that our daughters go to the same college? To which client should I give priority for my 5 p.m. slot? Do I wait until Monday to return this client's call? Do I cancel clients to see my son's play?

We are like tight rope walkers, finding a healthy balance at every step. Every day offers opportunities and challenges. Every day offers winds of change that challenge us to keep our balance. How do we handle it all?

I remember a gorgeous spring day, slightly warm with a cooling breeze, and about fifteen other adults walking as slow as snails. We were a pack of therapists learning about contemplative studies and the application of spirituality to mental health. Our teacher, a Zen monk, was leading us in a walking meditation.

Much of what we were studying was about how to ground ourselves and help our clients via the art of inner landscape awareness. I was mesmerized as our studies came to life with each mindful step. Akasha, our guide, asked us to balance on one leg, with the other leg crossed before us—as if we could sit back on a chair with our legs crossed in masculine fashion. We alternately struggled and succeeded with this goal.

Watching each of us find our place of balance, Akasha whispered into the spring air, "Every day of your lives is like this." I knew just what he meant: the beautiful details of our lives are found in the balance of each moment.

Reflection: At the end of the day, there is no more to be done. Be present to the end of your day. Know that tomorrow you'll have a chance to start again.

IMAGINE THAT

What: Connect yourself to happy feelings.

Imagine yourself in a favorite place, happy and peaceful. It could be a real place that you remember or it could be your ideal place of calm and bliss. Summon as many aspects of the place as possible, including sounds, smells, temperature, tastes, and visual details. Let these sensory cues come alive in your imagination and then bask in the glow of warm, happy sensations.

When: When you feel disconnected, anxious, spaced out, or melancholy.

Why: Summoning a happy place in your mind's eye allows you to revisit (or imagine) a place where you feel connected and alive. Your brain and body begin to respond as if you are there. You feel instantly at peace. Safe place imagery is widely used in working with individuals who have experienced trauma. In Eye Movement Desensitization Reprocessing (EMDR) protocol, safe place imagery is taught to clients as a way to de-escalate when they notice being caught in their emotions.

I learn a lot from my clients. I frequently receive unsolicited book recommendations, movie reviews, and new restaurant suggestions. I hear about where clients vacation, what news they know, and even what dog breeders they consult.

Sometimes I even learn from my client's previous therapists. On my intake form, I ask whether a new client has been in therapy before and if so, when and with whom. Occasionally I get a therapy newbie, but mostly I work with people who have had a few brushes (or more than a few) with the mental health field.

Some people cannot recall the name of their former therapists and tell me it was a waste of their time. (At this point, I usually send a silent blessing to the poor professional who tried his or her best). Other times, the new client glows when discussing past treatment. This was the case with Sarah, one of my first clients as a therapist. She said, "I absolutely loved my therapist in Minnesota. She was the wisest, smartest, most insightful person I've ever met."

"That's wonderful," I said, feeling myself shrink in her eyes (as I sent a silent blessing to myself that I might be remembered so fondly).

"In fact," Sarah continued, "she taught me the best instant soothing technique that I know."

I couldn't resist the temptation. "Really," I said, "tell me about it."

Sarah explained, "She told me about how to get to my happy place whenever I need to. It brings instant security."

"Your happy place? Do you mean like a visualization?" I inquired.

"Not just a visualization but a visitation . . . you really put yourself in the place and absorb it into your being. It feels wonderful and I use it all the time," she replied.

(I silently blessed this therapist whose happy place technique could now become part of my self-care and therapeutic cache.)

Upon making this technique my own, I found my favorite happy place in my memories of annual visits to Star Island, a tiny island ten miles off the coast of New Hampshire. I remember a warm, sunny spot on the rocks above the crashing waves, seagull sounds, and the smell of the sea. I love to visit this place in my mind's eye, especially on cold winter nights in New England.

Years later, when being trained in EMDR, I learned to help clients identify their safe/calm place as an initial phase in the EMDR protocol. I immediately recognized this tool as Sarah's former therapist's device. Now, I help clients claim their happy place at some point in our work together. It always produces a smile, for both of us.

Reflection: What is your favorite happy place to visit?

CHAPTER 6

PRACTICES FOR ENERGIZING

I WAS twenty-two years old when I moved to New York City. I didn't have a job, an apartment, or any idea what life as a grown-up might entail. I did, however, have a roommate and a whole lot of youthful hubris.

After securing a lease on a small studio apartment, I began my job search. Armed with an undergraduate liberal arts degree in psychology, I was qualified for . . . virtually nothing. One entry-level job led to another as I found myself frustrated with the mundane tasks of office life. Still, within a year I found a promising job in public relations.

Although I started as a glorified secretary, I had my eyes set on advancement. I measured my success by the presence or absence of a window in my office. One fateful night while out for dinner with a friend, he asked me about my future plans.

"What's your five year plan?" he probed, matter-of-factly.

I replied without hesitation, "My goal is to get a window office one day. But right now, all I want is to get my own cubicle. It's my primary mission."

As I walked home alone on 3rd Avenue, I found myself musing on whether or not my only mission was to improve my office status. Did it even matter what accounts I was working on? Did I care about the big pharmaceutical client or the candy company's image?

I found myself in an existential daze and my life unfolded into a blur of superficial and vacant goals. Something felt wrong. "Is this all there is to life?' I questioned.

Crestfallen and uncertain, I took my vacation days to visit a summer camp called Ghost Ranch in the hills of Albuquerque, NM. On the third day, under a brilliant and clear sky, I took a hike up a mountain called Kitchen Mesa. . At the top, tired and desperate for direction, I looked skyward, beseeching the heavens. "What should I do with my life?" I said aloud.

In the silence of the open air, just me and the billowing clouds, I sensed my whole life's experience align with that single moment. I felt or heard or intuited a voice that said quite clearly, "You need to help people in emotional pain."

So that was it. I felt a call and subsequently changed the direction of my life. I went home and applied right away to programs in social work. I began classes that very autumn and instantly felt at home. Once I began working with clients, I knew I had indeed found meaningful work, work that made a difference in my life and the lives of others. I had found my purpose. And I didn't care about my office or whether or not I had a window.

What was your moment when you knew you wanted to become a therapist? Each of us took the first step on this career path, and then the next. Can you remember the feeling of choosing this path?

Over two and half decades since my mountaintop moment, I sometimes forget the initial enthusiasm that propelled me into the field of psychotherapy. Years of facing the realities of billing, quotas, Medicaid audits, CEU requirements, malpractice insurance, session notes, insurance rules, procedure codes, staff meetings, and client frustrations have, at times, created powerful distractions from my inner purpose. In the face of the hard realities of our profession, we are all susceptible to burnout. That freshness of purpose that once was our momentum can begin to feel very foreign.

And for some, indeed, the momentum for counseling may be gone. We are all irrevocably changed by the work we do and we must honor that change. But to move forward, day in and day out, propelled by the force of stress and habit alone, is to neither honor change nor the truth of your work's purpose. There's a reason why you entered this field, a reason why you answered your own call and decided this was important, meaningful work. If you are reading this book, I suspect that inner purpose is still there, deep down. It is the light that will illuminate your work and the light that will guide you in taking care of yourself.

Connecting with your purpose for doing this work will go a long way in helping you feel positive, motivated, and energized. Victor Frankl, author of *Man's Search for Meaning*, quotes Nietzsche as writing, "He who has a why to live for can bear almost any how."

The practices in this section also address the physical side to feeling energetic and alive in your work. As therapists, we spend a great deal of time in low energy contexts, sitting silently in our chairs and moving gently about our work environments. The micro-self-care practices that follow are a mix of those designed to get your body moving (to renew your energy) and to help you plug back in to your higher purpose (to renew your spirit).

Get ready for your mind, body, and spirit to wake up!

HELPING HANDS

What: Renew your personal mission as a helper.

As a method to center yourself around your mission and energize your day with purpose, begin with some or all of the following steps:

1. Place both of your hands on your head and say, "May the spirit of healing be in my thoughts."
2. Place your hands over your eyes and say, "May I see with clarity."
3. Place your hands over your ears and say, "May I hear what needs to be heard."
4. Place your hands over your mouth and say, "May words of healing flow from my lips."
5. Place your hands over your heart and say, "May my heart be open to those who suffer."
6. Lastly, hold your arms out, hands opened, and say, "May my hands be of service to those in need."

When: At the beginning of your work day.

Why: Like the Hippocratic oath, still recited by physicians around the world, this self-care tool will help you focus your attention on your clients, renew the spirit of your ethical obligation, and energize your enthusiasm for your day's work. This ritual-like practice endows your work with greater energy and a sense of importance while using physical movements to embody and internalize the spirit and mission of your work.

Do you have a favorite professional conference? It might be a conference that reflects your degree: the annual APA (American Psychological Association) or AAMFT (American Association for Marriage and Family Therapy) conference. It might be a specialty conference that draws you year after year, such as an EFT (Emotionally Focused Couple Therapy), grief, addictions, or trauma conference. Or you may have a preference for a long-standing general conference, such as the Psychotherapy Networker Symposium (three decades running).

I have been to many wonderful conferences but my personal favorite was the NICABM conference (National Institute for the Clinical Application of Behavioral Medicine) in Hilton Head, SC. When Ruth Buczynski ended this face-to-face conference and shifted to online education, it was a sad day for many. At the final conference, the keynote talks really caught my attention. I remember, in particular, that a prominent physician shared a ritual with which she began her mornings. Placing her hands on parts of her body, she sent out her requests: "May I help heal others . . . may I listen . . . may I see clearly . . . may I speak kindly . . . may my heart be open."

People around me were touched and moved by these tender words. I heard sniffles—a string had been plucked in our hearts. There was something so simple about the words and yet so meaningful.

As with many fabulous conferences, I left with pages of notes and handouts along with the glow of learning and connecting with my colleagues. Sadly, as time went by, I forgot much of what I had learned. The physician's simple ritual, however, stayed with me long past the conference.

I have since adopted it as my daily favorite and have felt the power of its invocation. Whether you are speaking to your higher power, the universe, or your best self, this micro-self-care practice will empower you to do your best work.

Reflection: How would your workday be different if you embodied the awesome privilege of being a healer?

ANGEL WINGS

What: Look to a symbol of comfort for calm and renewed confidence.

Put a symbol of peace and well being up high in your office or in an unobtrusive place that only you can see. You may choose a small (an inch or smaller) angel pin, meaningful crystal, small figurine, or article from nature. You might find a place above a door, between some books, or just peeking from somewhere on your desk.

When: During a session, whenever you're feeling uncertain or disheartened.

Purpose: As therapists, we have very firm and clear boundaries between our personal beliefs and our relationships with clients. At the same time, it is our deepest personal beliefs about ourselves, our place in the universe, and the meaning of life that bring us to do our work and sustain us in our mission. Thus, the work we do is highly spiritual, however you may conceive of the word. This micro-self-care practice is a nod to the importance of allowing our guiding beliefs to sustain and companion us as we strive to offer our best selves to our clients.

During my second social work internship, I worked in Brooklyn at The Jewish Board of Family and Children's Services. It was a plum internship and I was thrilled to be working there. Known as an excellent placement, they offered interesting cases, thorough in-service training, fantastic supervision, and a climate of excellence. It felt like heaven.

That is, until I made a colossal and very embarrassing mistake. I had a caseload that included children and families. Of course, being inexperienced, I wasn't exactly sure what I was doing at any given time. I knew, at least, how to take detailed chart notes, which were of course reviewed by my supervisor.

It was during a consultation meeting when my supervisor brought a mistake to my attention. She opened the chart of Bobby and pointed out that I had written some incriminating comments in two different session notes. The first: "Bobby had multiple bruises up and down his arms. When I asked him what they were from, he told me he had been rough housing with his brother." The second, "Bobby had a burn mark on his upper lip. His mother told me he had been burned by a hot pan."

My supervisor mentioned that I should have brought these issues to her attention immediately. She stressed that we were under legal obligation to report any suspected child abuse to Child Protective Services. She reminded me that, if audited, a lack of professional follow-up could get the agency into trouble.

Still more disconcerting was the issue of poor Bobby. Was he being abused at home? Had I completely missed it? Was I naïve to record his injuries yet accept the excuses? I felt afraid for Bobby, his family, and the system he was about to enter. "What should I do in the next session?" I asked.

My supervisor explained how to report this client to the state and then how to relay that information to the client. And then, my supervisor, who happened to be a student of the *Course in Miracles*, asked me how I felt about angels.

"I suppose I like them well enough," I replied.

She told me that ever since she had been practicing in the field (some thirty years at that point), she had kept an angel figure somewhere in her office. She kept it virtually hidden, in the folds of drapery or on the top of a door. Only she was aware of its presence.

"When I feel overwhelmed or I'm really not sure what to do next," she told me, "I look to my angel and I ask for help with the case."

"Does it help?" I asked.

"I'm not sure I always get an immediate answer, but I'm quite certain that it doesn't hurt to connect with Spirit," she replied.

I have to admit that in each of my eight subsequent offices I have kept a discreet angel. When I'm feeling a bit stymied, I glance up at my angel and ask for a little backup. And sometimes, I simply ask the angels to shower a few blessings on this person who is suffering. And on me too, while they're at it.

I like to think that helpers are doing angels' work.

Reflection: What symbol of peace, love, or companionship might support you in your most difficult hours?

BOW AND ARROW

What: Remind yourself that change doesn't always feel forward moving.

Put your arms in the position of launching an arrow with a bow. Tilt your head back a bit to expose your neck and open up your chest by pulling the 'bow' wider apart. Switch sides and repeat in the other direction.

When: Before or after a session when you're feeling frustrated (or demoralized) about a client's lack of progress.

Why: This micro-self-care practice is a method for embodying and internalizing a more open understanding of change. It can feel frustrating to work with a client when progress seems slow or halted. You may feel downright ineffective or inadequate as a helping professional. It can help to frame slow progress or seeming setbacks in a broader perspective of growth. Much in the way putting a smile on your face can stimulate happiness, holding a posture with your head high, shoulders back and chest expanded can generate an attitude of confidence and courage. Remember, like the arrow that pulls backwards before launching forwards, our clients often take a step back before taking two steps forward.

Charles was absolutely beside himself. He looked as if an earthquake, tsunami, or lightning bolt had struck him. He and his wife of twenty-five years sat on my couch. Sheila had her head down. Charles had already told me on the intake call that he had recently discovered Sheila's affairs.

Sheila had left up her computer screen with a sexy message to another man. When Charles found it, he initially thought it was some kind of joke. Sheila eventually confessed she had been having an affair for the past six months and that she had also had a short affair ten years ago. Charles was dumbfounded. He claimed he never saw this coming. They had raised children together. They had a new grandchild. How could this happen?

Sheila was contrite, sheepish, and apologetic. She said she was willing to do whatever it took to save their marriage and have Charles forgive her. The next week, however, Sheila acted frustrated that Charles wasn't moving on. She said Charles was dwelling on her affairs and couldn't get past them. I explained that Charles had experienced a huge trauma, that it would take time for him to process the betrayal and grieve the end of the marriage he knew. Together, they would need to put down the building blocks for a new marriage. It would most certainly not be a quick fix.

At their next session, Sheila seemed even more impatient and suggested she and Charles separate for a while. Every discussion seemed to dissolve into a rehashing of her two affairs. Charles was shocked that Sheila would even suggest a separation. She must want out of the marriage, he worried.

I explained to them that sometimes, in a process of growth, we have to move seemingly backwards before we can move forwards. I demonstrated with an invisible bow and arrow. "The arrow goes backwards in order to gain the momentum it needs to move forwards." I said. Although Charles was not particularly consoled, they agreed that Sheila would temporarily stay with a friend.

Honestly, I wasn't sure if this turn of events was a new beginning or the end of their marriage. But as they left the session that afternoon, I did my own *bow and arrow* stretch to remind myself that the paths of change are not always as they seem.

This couple did reunite after a month. Sheila came to realize she was willing to fight for the marriage and Charles became willing to let go of his daily punishment of Sheila. Gradually, their love for each other and their long history provided the scaffolding to rebuild their relationship.

Reflection: Notice whether an embodied awareness of the multidirectional nature of change helps you feel more patient with the therapeutic process.

MAKING SENSE

What: Heighten awareness of your external senses.

Use your hand to guide you on a tour of your five senses. Sit in a chair and hold your hand open in your lap. Following your five senses one by one, sensitize your awareness to the present moment. Use the pattern 'SSSTT': Close your thumb to indicate **sight** and focus your attention, without naming or judging, on an intricate visual detail. Let your eyes follow its contour, noticing what you've never noticed before. Then, closing your pointer finger, listen to the **sounds** around you. Can you notice the silence between the sounds? Close your middle finger to indicate **smell**. Feel your in-breath as it passes your upper lip and cools your nostril. Are aromas present? Next, close your ring finger to indicate **touch**, feel your body in the chair and, feel the air on your face, noting the sensation of your clothes against your skin. Finally, closing your pinky, move your attention to your **tongue**. Notice any tingling, the neutral taste of your saliva, memories of your last meal across your taste buds. Stay still for a moment just taking in the uniqueness and wonder of the multi-sensory moment.

When: In the middle of your workday.

Why: Siegel, in his book, *The Mindful Therapist*, argues that mindfulness training builds neurological resilience and flexibility, two necessary characteristics for the healthy and effective therapist. Short mindfulness practices such as this not only still busy thoughts and calm the nervous system in the moment, but also strengthen new neural pathways. Over time, your capacity for arriving in the moment and staying aware increases.

Eckart Tolle has a beautiful description of sensory presence, a quality that we want to cultivate in our therapy rooms (1999, p. 96):

> Presence is needed to become aware of the beauty, the majesty, the sacredness of nature. Have you ever gazed up into the infinity of space on a clear night, awestruck by the absolute stillness and inconceivable vastness of it? Have you listened, truly listened, to the sound of a mountain stream in the forest? Or the song of a blackbird at dusk on a quiet summer evening? . . . You have to put down for a moment your personal baggage of problems, of past and future, as well as all your knowledge: otherwise, you will see but not see, hear but not hear.

The micro-self-care practices *Now Hear This*, and *Lavender Fields* are mindful awareness practices that focus attentions on single sense awareness. You may find that your awareness is enabled more with one sense than another. However, *Making Sense* asks you to broaden your awareness to all stimuli, using your fingers as a guide.

Eric and I had been working together for just over a year. He had originally come for assistance in dealing with post-divorce depression. He had made progress but his symptoms had recently been triggered at the funeral of his Aunt. Although we had never discussed it in great detail, he had been sexually abused by his Aunt when he was eleven years old. Going to the funeral and hearing people talk about how wonderful she was caused a flood of feelings. He began to have nightmares.

I was fresh off of my EMDR (Eye Movement Desensitization Reprocessing) trauma training and I felt he would be a good candidate for this modality. We started with Eric's most recent trigger event. Using bilateral stimulation, my fingers moved repetitively from right to left in front of his eyes. He began floating back in time, sifting through memories—one leading to the next in a cascade of free association. Over the next thirty minutes, Eric moved from a reported distress level of '10' (with 10 being maximum distress and 0 being no distress) to a '1'. Eric left feeling hopeful and relaxed.

I sat in my chair in the quiet of the room. Even as I was impressed with the power of my hand, I felt drained. The effort of using a new intervention, of hearing the intensity of Eric's traumatic memories, and of exercising my left arm so vigorously had left me in a mild state of disassociation from my external senses.

I needed to come into the present moment and renew my dual awareness before my next session. Staring down at my hand, I experienced my own free association. I remembered a self-care workshop in which the leader, Alaya Chadwick, suggested that our hands hold the key to our sensory self-care. Our hands being ever present, we can use our fingers to cue us to our senses—five fingers, five senses.

I spent the next few minutes focusing on each of my external senses using my fingers to guide me. Tuning into my senses helped me come to my senses.

Reflection: Can you feel a fresh source of energy when you begin to take in and pay attention to the sensory details that you've been missing?

MARCHING ORDERS

What: Wake yourself up with movement.

Stand to attention with back straight and head erect. March in place, bringing your legs up and down while swinging your arms. Keep marching for thirty seconds while you say, "I am awake and ready. I am awake and ready." For added benefit, add a few twists, putting your right elbow toward your left knee and then your left elbow to your right knee as you march.

When: In the afternoon when your energy starts to slump.

Why: Psychotherapy involves a lot of sitting. It is critically important for your mood and physical well being to move and stretch several times a day. Increased heart rate and taking in short breaths through your nose stimulate your sympathetic nervous system, helping you feel more awake, alert, and positive. This activity quickly gets your blood flowing. Lift your legs high to stretch your hamstrings, giving your lower back a rest. The combined words and movement give your body and mind a boost of energy.

It was my first trip to India. I had traveled there with my dear friend Martha on a spiritual pilgrimage. Each morning after our breakfast, we walked two miles from our guest house to the ashram for mid-morning meditation.

I found each morning's walk fascinating and even more enjoyable than the meditations. I never knew what we might encounter. Monkeys and cows strolling through the streets were commonplace, but the monkey on the back of a bike was quite a surprise. We passed children playing who waved enthusiastically. We passed men in huts, diligently ironing clothes. We passed women in stunning, flowing, colorful saris carrying huge jugs or baskets on their heads.

One morning, on our way to meditation, we were met with crowds of people and festivities. Celebrating the national spring festival of colors, *Holi*, participants threw intensely colored powders on all passersby. A blizzard of neon colors exploded in a riot of celebration. By the time we arrived to the ashram, we were drenched in color.

Having entered at the ashram, our leader asked us to stand beside our cushions. The customary way to begin a meditation was to engage in yogic breathing exercises and poses to stretch and calm the body. This morning, however, I could feel the heightened and playful holiday energy all around me.

"Today," said our leader, "we must work with the celebratory energy around us. To prepare for our meditation, we must let the joy flow within us." We followed him in an exuberant march, booming the words, "I am awake and ready. I am awake and ready."

The fifty people in the room threw their arms up in rhythm to their rising knees. We were indeed all awake, colorful, and ready for whatever adventure the day had to offer.

Reflection: Notice how your body feels after short, vigorous movement. Can you feel a shift in energy and alertness?

ASHES TO ASHES

What: Strengthen your feelings of gratitude for life.

Spend several minutes reflecting on impermanence by gazing at an object and thinking these words: "This object has come and it will go. I have come and I will go." Notice as you sit that each moment is slightly different than the next. Finish by placing your hand over your heart and thinking the words, "I savor the present moment. I choose to live my life while it lasts." Let your awareness of death energize your experience of life.

When: When you've had an unexpected cancellation or have become otherwise aware of the inevitability of change and loss.

Why: Reflecting on impermanence is perhaps a tall order. It can feel like a painful, in-your-face wake-up call. Many of our clients share their experience of impermanence that results from lost loved ones, divorce, financial losses, and old age. Yet by keeping professional distance, we too easily move on with the business of our lives without personal reflection. Avoiding the reality of impermanence may lead to taking life for granted.

Buddhists have long known that making friends with impermanence is a way to reduce suffering. In *Living as a River*, a wonderful book on the nature of impermanence and coping with change, Bodhipaksa writes, "But such is how we deal with fear: we cling, sometimes blindly . . . Clinging is a strategy for dealing with change, but it is also a strategy that is woven through with denial, and that isn't very effective" (2010). Reflecting on whether your attachment to the fixed nature of things fuels your denial of impermanence can allow you to heighten your sense of presence and make life's moments more precious.

"This week, your homework is to reflect on your own impermanence." The words leapt off the page of my Buddhist study class homework sheet. We were advised to open our hearts and let the awareness of our eminent demise be our inspiration.

I was not new to this Buddhist perspective. I had read Buddhist texts that graphically focused on rotting corpses. I owned mala beads made from yak and camel bones, a reminder of our own mortality. I had witnessed Tibetan monks labor for weeks over an intricate sand mandala and then sweep it into a river, a ritual to symbolize impermanence.

As a grief counselor I have been no stranger to death and loss. I've learned to never assume that a person will live a 'normal' lifespan. I have heard too many stories of babies, toddlers, young children, adolescents, young adults, and middle-aged loved ones all dying 'before their time.'

Yet, even with death always on my horizon, the homework of reflecting on my own impermanence produced a bigger *gulp* than I expected. You'd think that having crossed the half-century mark, I'd be more aware that the grim reaper is looking over my shoulder. When things are going well it is simply easy to forget that life has an expiration date.

It so happened that I found myself tackling this Buddhist homework while on a silent retreat in the hermitages of an Episcopalian guesthouse (holding my rosary beads next to my mala beads). As I sat with the uncomfortable yet freeing reflections of my own impermanence, I learned that these very hermitages where I had sought refuge for over a dozen years were slated to be torn down.

Oh no! How can it be? I thought. I struggled with feelings of loss and anger. Yet, as I went into my reflection on my own impermanence and the impermanence of my hermitage, my fear of loss was replaced by the thought, *Everything is impermanent. The hermitage is here today and soon gone. I am here today and soon gone.*

And so, the hermitage and I, doomed as we both were in our present forms, opened to a brilliant blue sky and rested in peace. Making friends with death, like facing any of the hard stuff, is indeed so much better than living with fear. Facing the inevitable with an open heart to the present moment engenders a kind of freedom paired with contentment.

Reflection: Are you willing to find the gifts embedded in reflection of your own impermanence?

WORK IN THE WORLD

What: Saturate yourself with gratitude.

Think of three things that you're grateful for about your employment. List them in your mind, one at a time. Imagine how life would be if you were unemployed. Notice and be glad for the good things at this moment in your work life.

When: When you're on your way to work—by car, train, subway, or foot.

Why: Gratitude is a direct pathway to happiness. A daily gratitude practice will boost your happiness levels. Intentionally redirecting your mind toward gratitude is a way to build new neural structures in the brain that support feeling contented. It's not too grandiose to declare that this directed attention practice will not only increase your job satisfaction but also your life satisfaction. As it improves your mood and elevates your optimism, it will make you a more effective therapist.

It was a bitter winter day in New England when I emerged from the subway station in Harvard Yard and walked eight blocks to the St. John of the Evangelist monastery. I was attending a talk by my favorite of the monks, Brother Curtis.

I had been attending spiritual retreats with the SSJE brothers since 2002. This was a half-day talk on the topic of gratitude. Brother Curtis spoke so eloquently about the grace of gratitude and how it can transform one's relationship to life that I gently wept.

He shared his personal story about having been a parish

priest in his thirties, but feeling as if something was missing in his life. Visiting this SSJE monastery one day, while on retreat, he instantly knew he had come home and subsequently entered a monastic life. He loved the rhythm of prayer, his community of brothers, and his daily devotion to God. Every day he gives thanks for the life he leads and the work he does.

When he finished his story, he said with a twinkle in his eye, "I invite you to look at your life's work, to view what you do through the lens of extreme gratitude. Perhaps you will one day have a different job, but today you have the work you have. Give thanks for it. Savor gratitude for what you are doing, how you are doing it, and with whom you are doing it. Give thanks every day and it will fill you to overflowing."

His words were so simple, pure, and spot-on.

When I struggle with the dissatisfaction of certain aspects of my work, I look back to that sense of spontaneous gratitude in my early career. I had secured a highly coveted internship at the Jewish Board of Family and Children Services. Whenever I took the subway to Brooklyn Heights, I would think about how lucky I was to have such a plumb internship, a great supervisor, and colleagues I enjoyed. Every time I opened the door to that office, I was infused with a sense of gratitude for being there.

Gratitude makes you happier. It improves your well being. As Brother Curtis said, "Don't start your day without taking stock of your work in the world—and be glad for it."

Reflection: What would you miss if you didn't work in your current setting or if you left the field altogether?

HAPPY DANCE

What: Improve your mood and increase your energy.

Stand on the balls of your feet and gently bounce up and down. This is low impact—you're not jumping. Rock up and down on the balls of your feet. Breathe deeply as you first go slowly and then more quickly and then slowly again. Add a smile on your lips as you gently bounce for thirty seconds.

When: Between client sessions.

Why: Like many of the energizing practices in this section, this tool relies on movement and breath to trigger the sympathetic nervous system and move aerated blood to your limbs and brain. Intentionally forming a smile on your face is a form of facial mirroring; you are mirroring what a happy person's face looks like. Our ability to shift our emotions by mimicry is not only easily experienced but has been demonstrated in research (e.g., Hess and Blairy, 2001). Enjoy this playful bounce as you lift your mood higher and higher.

Each morning that we came into the workshop, our leader was gently bouncing on the balls of his feet. He smiled a wide Cheshire cat grin and stopped shortly after the couples assembled on their mats.

This was a Valentine's weekend retreat in Thai massage for couples—equal parts massage, stretching, and yoga. We were an assortment of young and older couples. Each of us had come for a weekend of connection, rekindling, and togetherness.

We had introduced ourselves in the beginning—the empty nester couple, the lesbian newlyweds, the couple who had just celebrated fifty years together. However, there wasn't much interaction between the couples. Mostly we stayed on our mats and followed instructions, primarily placing our partner's limbs in different pretzel combinations.

We listened intently to the teacher and his diverse and interesting stories. We heard about his withholding mother who claimed "most people hug too much." We learned about his subsequent deep desire for touch, which led him to become an expert in body work. We heard about the secrets of Thai massage and its lessons for better living.

But on the last day he still hadn't explained the bouncing behavior that greeted us each morning. A shy empty nester finally asked, "What is it that you're doing when we walk in the room?"

"Oh this?" he said, and he began to demonstrate, all the while smiling and bouncing. "This is the happy dance."

We were surprised. We had been listening to this man's stream of consciousness for two and half straight days—his secrets to better living, lessons from ancient masters—and he had never bothered to tell us about the *happy dance*?

"Oh yes," he said, "Actually, if you don't remember anything else from this weekend, then just remember the happy dance. Bounce like this, while smiling and breathing deeply, every morning for at least a minute, and you will dramatically improve your happiness levels. I learned this from a Tibetan lama in India."

And as it turns out, it is the only pose that I actually remember from that weekend without consulting my notes. Fortunately, I've discovered, it works.

Reflection: Do you notice a difference in your day if you start it off with intentional happiness?

SING A SONG OF SIXPENCE

What: Lift your spirits with a song.

Sing a fun song. Think back on songs that you loved when you were a kid, teenager, or young adult. Perhaps you remember a verse from a favorite campfire song such as "Oh Suzanna." Or maybe a holiday classic, "Dashing through the snow, in a one horse open sleigh . . ." Do you have a favorite oldie but goodie? A favorite song by the Beatles? Anything by Johnny Cash? How about "Somewhere Over the Rainbow"?

When: When you are driving in the car to or from work.

Why: Micro-self-care is about attending to yourself with kindness. Consider each song you sing a gift to yourself. Singing lifts up your spirit and connects you to a different level of feeling and awareness. In using your voice, you lift your head to a posture of confidence and energize yourself with deeper breaths. But most of all, singing a favorite song associated with good memories stimulates the feelings associated with happy times. No one is listening—give yourself the gift of song.

We shuffled quietly into the small room. A frail woman, in her eighties, was lying under a colorful afghan. She didn't stir as the eight of us gathered at the foot of her hospital bed.

This was a hospice house and we were a band of hospice singers. We sang to the dying as a kind of ministry—the ministry of music.

The woman's daughter, a middle-aged version of the woman in the bed, had told us in the hallway that her mother had only days if not hours left on this planet. She had been largely unconscious for the past few days. She was a deeply religious woman and was not afraid to die.

First we sang "Blue Moon" to the inert figure. Then we sang, "Sentimental Journey." We knew that music touched our listeners even when they didn't look at us or flatter us with applause. We could tell that the daughter was moved by our efforts.

Then, as we began to sing, "In the Garden," a classic Christian hymn, I noticed that the woman with one foot in this world and one in the next raised her eyebrow. She moved her fingers, and by the time we sang the chorus, "And He walked with me and He talked with me . . ." she was mouthing the words.

I glanced at the other singers. They were mesmerized by the song's effect on this woman, who now seemed to glow with reverent energy.

Wrapping up with "Amazing Grace," I noticed that not only did each of my fellow singers have tears streaming down their cheeks, but so did this dear, dying woman. She never opened her eyes but we knew she had been touched by song.

Although I have been a singer all of my life, this was when I really understood the transformative power of music.

Reflection: What mood is evoked for you when you sing?

MAKE 'EM LAUGH

What: Use laughter as mood medicine.

Have a joke book, or go online and bookmark comedy websites and/or funny videos. Find things to make you chuckle. Maybe it's a *Saturday Night Live* skit or a book of limericks. When friends send you images and short videos that make you laugh, save them to a special "laughter" file.

When: In the afternoon, when you have a few moments between clients.

Why: The benefits of laughter have been chronicled since Norman Cousins, in his *Anatomy of an Illness*, discussed how watching Marx Brothers movies helped cure him of cancer. Continuous laughter is an aerobic exercise; it oxygenates your blood and stretches muscles all over your body. Quite simply, it's a mood lifter. It's hard to laugh and feel down simultaneously. As therapists, we know that mood is fickle. The slight stimulation of a thought or emotion, a gentle shift in body chemistry or blood sugar, a change in weather, or a disturbing story can trigger wide swings in mood. Laughter is a self-soothing practice that will enhance your mood. Take it on with intention. It's good medicine.

My four-person consultation group had been hit hard. Each of us had had our own personal challenge. For me, my husband had just finished six months of arduous chemotherapy, a huge stressor in our family. Although his prognosis was optimistic, the months of chemotherapy had been devastating.

For Gina, she had been diagnosed with ovarian cancer and was actively undergoing chemotherapy, radiation, and alternative supplemental treatments. She was wearing a wig and had been Skyping in to our consultation meetings when she felt up to it. The rest of us were stunned by her sickness and frightened by her less than optimistic prognosis.

Poor Rachel, who had recently finished having both of her knees replaced, had just finished a long recovery period and was now facing a major back surgery. She had all but given up her private practice.

And Susan's best friend was battling a malignant brain tumor and had been given three months to live. Her mother and mother-in-law had died recently and Susan felt that everyone around her was either sick, dying, or both.

Perhaps we were a typical slice of middle-aged life in America. After all, if you live long enough, you're bound to face all kinds of suffering and death. But we were feeling unusually vulnerable and weak. It had been a long time since any of us had had particularly good news, either personally or professionally.

At one of our meetings during these hard times, a day when the energy in the room was palpably heavy, Susan suddenly announced, "We *need* to laugh. I think it's mandatory right now." She pulled out her tablet and said, "I think we should spend our consultation time finding funny videos."

We nodded our consent, not really feeling lighthearted. But Susan pulled up Marx Brothers classics, clips from *America's Funniest Home Videos*, and other comedy routines. Still reluctantly chuckling from the previous video, I asked, "Have you seen the one with the talking dog?" Susan shook her head "No." "You know," I prompted, "'The Ultimate Dog Tease'? It's my all time favorite funny video." I've seen it probably thirty times but together we all came unglued with laughter as we watched. Suddenly we were a bunch of giggling schoolgirls.

All four of us therapists, feeling wounded by our current life circumstances, spent an hour in sidesplitting laughter. It was probably one of our best—and most healing—meetings ever.

Reflection: Notice the shift in your mood and energy of your body once you spend a few minutes laughing.

STARFISH

What: Calm your nerves by connecting to something larger than yourself.

Put your hand over your heart, and say or think the words, "I am going to touch a life today. I'm going to say something that someone especially needs to hear. May I be of service."

When: Before you make a presentation or a speech, teach a class, lead a workshop, or address any type of audience.

Why: This tool helps to minimize performance anxiety or nerves. When you are sharing your skills or information with a group of people, it's important to put your ego in the back seat. Remember that you are providing a service (even if you're getting paid to give the talk). Get out of your own way and know that you will say something that will make a difference to someone in your audience. As therapists, we are accustomed to helping one person at a time. Remembering this as you stand before a group will engender a sense of humility that is the antidote to jitters.

Have you ever heard the Jerry Seinfeld joke regarding the study that claimed people's number one fear is public speaking, with the number two being fear of death? Seinfeld quipped, "This means to the average person, if you have to be at a funeral, you'd rather be in the casket than doing the eulogy."

When I made my official public speaking debut, I was thirty years old and had volunteered to give an adult education talk at my church regarding the topic of grief. I was researching my first book, *Transcending Loss*, at the time and was hoping to share some of my ideas. I was terrified, shaking in my proverbial boots.

Because I've been a singer and performer all of my life, I was accustomed to being 'on stage.' But I wasn't accustomed to being 'off script.' Armed with my note cards and a microphone, I proceeded to share my findings about losses of all kinds and the possibility of transformation. Afterwards, I received favorable reviews, but it was one woman in particular whose response stayed with me.

She came up to me and said, "Everything you just explained describes my experience with breast cancer. I see now that a part of me died with that diagnosis, and now I'm transforming into a new self. Thank you so much for helping me see that so clearly." I was blown away. I hadn't even been talking about breast cancer and yet she had made the information personally relevant to her own life situation.

Since that time, I have given hundreds of talks—community events, book readings, professional conferences, workshops, seminars, and online classes. I always get a bit nervous before each event, but I also know that whether I have an audience of ten or two hundred, there is at least one person in that audience who needs to hear something I'm going to say. Whether I get feedback or not, I always know that my words have reached the ears of at least one person who needed to hear them.

I'm reminded of the boy and the starfish story. When a man watched a boy's hopeless task of returning thousands of stranded starfish to the sea he said, "You can't make a difference." The boy replied as he continued to throw starfish into the sea one at a time, "I made a difference to this starfish . . . and this one."

We are masters of affecting one life at a time. Whether in the therapy room or in front of an audience, let yourself serve people and touch lives, one at a time.

Reflection: Do you believe you have something to share that will matter to even one person, something that will make a difference?

STRONG AND SOFT

What: Cope with the suffering you witness.

Think to yourself the words, "Strong back," and simultaneously sink your belly button back to your spine as you exhale. Then think to yourself the words, "Soft front," and simultaneously expand your stomach (like a balloon filling with air) as you inhale. You can do this discretely during a session.

When: When you are present with deep suffering or feel you failed a client in some critical way. You can do this either after such a session or even during.

Why: This micro-self-care practice is adapted from a meditation by Joan Halifax in her amazing book, *Being with the Dying*. As we bring awareness to both our strength and vulnerability, it fosters a state of equanimity. Through this practice, we summon the skills of courage and compassion as we allow ourselves to be fully present with suffering and even death. As humans we have the innate ability to mirror and experience the emotions of others. As counselors we must walk the fine line between accurate empathy and vicarious suffering. The latter leads to vicarious trauma, the former to good therapy. Bringing attention to our body posture and breath, we recalibrate awareness of our emotional arousal even as we remain open to our client. Furthermore, working with the idea of strength and simultaneous vulnerability reminds us that we are human in our limited capacity to help. Knowing this helps us be gentler with ourselves.

"If you're in this field long enough, you *will* have a client commit suicide," he said slowly and methodically. I still remember these words from a supervisor when I was new to the work. He continued, "You must not be too hard on yourself when it happens. Be diligent and do your best work, but if someone really wants to exit this planet, you cannot stop them."

I recollected his warning as my client sat across from me, reaching for a tissue, her eyes full of tears, saying, "I don't know how it happened."

Josephine, a woman in her thirties, was a mental health counselor whose sixteen-year-old client had taken her own life the previous week. Josephine recounted the moment she learned of Clarissa's sad fate. "Clarissa had definitely been sullen in our last session. She was talking about the pressure of final exams and how everyone seemed to be handling it better than she was." Josephine shook her head. "I don't know how I missed it. Suicide wasn't even on my radar."

A friend of the family had called Josephine to tell her the news. Clarissa's mother wasn't up to making calls but wanted Josephine to know that Clarissa wouldn't be coming to any more sessions. She had been found by her father, hanging in the shower.

Josephine looked like she might be sick and she started to cry harder. "That poor girl. I completely failed her. Maybe I shouldn't even be a counselor."

My work with Josephine was short term, helping her to come to grips with the shock of losing a client, the feeling that she had failed, the reality that she could be sued, and her own lack of confidence in her career.

I shared with her the words of my former supervisor and together we practiced the *strong and soft* self-care tool. Originally presented in the context of helpers who sit with the dying, this self-care practice forces a deep breath and stimulates inner body awareness in a way that allows us to be moved by deep suffering (others and our own) without being overwhelmed.

We are all in the process of dying, of facing irrevocable change one day after another. This perspective feels melancholy at first, but there is a rising of compassionate equanimity that comes with its contemplation.

Reflection: Can you forgive yourself for not being omniscient and omnipotent? Can you stay present with suffering and not need fix it?

PUPPET STRINGS

What: Reduce your in-session drowsiness (or daydreaming).

Imagine a string at the top of your head and now imagine it pulling you upwards, causing you to lengthen your spine and loosen your neck. With your lips closed, lift your soft palette (as if you have an egg inside your mouth). This sometimes induces a yawn, which, paradoxically will wake you up rather than make you sleepier.

When: When you feel drowsy in a session, perhaps are even nodding off, and need a quick wake up fix.

Why: Yawning increases oxygen in your blood and to your brain by giving your lungs a boost of air. Erect posture signals to your body that you are awake and ready. Redirecting your mind to body awareness and intentionally adjusting your posture reestablishes a sense of control and cues your body to be alert.

Let's face it—any time in a session is an inopportune moment to begin snoring. I have never actually fallen asleep during a session, thank heavens. I've come close however, and have certainly been guilty of getting sleepy or distracted with a client, especially after a big lunch.

Once upon a time, a woman came to see me devastated that her husband had recently left her. She was grieving the end of her marriage and the end of her dream that they would live out their golden years together.

She told me about their long marriage and how she was

shocked when he came up to her and said, "I think we should get divorced." She shook her head, tearing up. "An earthquake would have been less surprising," she said. I was listening, following her story and then, I think I missed a word or two. I began thinking about my evening plans. *What did she just say?* I wondered.

I could tell that my client didn't notice my attention lapse because she continued to talk as if nothing was wrong with me. I felt like I was in a *Peanuts* cartoon listening to Charlie Brown's teacher, "blah, blah blah, blah blah." I crossed my legs and felt myself starting to shrink.

Suddenly, a higher level of self-awareness clicked in and I heard the voice of my childhood choir director, Mr. Hermonaut, saying, "Posture . . . *good* posture . . . is the key to everything. When in doubt, sit up straight." He was right. Good posture seemed to improve everything.

And so, I sat up straight, opened my jaw, and stifled a yawn. My distraction didn't completely disappear but I had reduced my drowsiness and awakened my dual awareness. Now, conscious of my inner world and the presenting circumstances, I listened carefully. *I can do this*, I thought.

Happily I was awake when she said she was relieved that she came to see me and already felt better. I definitely don't want to sleep through any compliments.

Reflection: Notice your posture in session. Are you getting sleepy? Maybe you could use a little lift.

FRESH AIR FUND

What: Reinvigorate yourself during a long day.

Go outside and repeat the following pattern three times: sniff in through your nose twice, breathe out quickly through your mouth twice: "Sniff, sniff, ha, ha." Follow three rounds of breathing by touching or looking at some detail of nature—a tree trunk, leaf, flower, or cloud.

When: When you have a break after several clients.

Why: Quick, repetitive breaths are energizing. They oxygenate your blood and stimulate your nervous system. We also thrive when we come in contact with nature. It uplifts, inspires, and reminds us there is a bigger context than our own little, egoic world. Paying attention to the natural world brings us into a feeling of greater connection to the rich and ever changing energy of life. If trees speak to helpers everywhere, perhaps Mary Oliver has heard it right:

> "It's simple," they say,
> "and you too have come
> into the world to do this, to go easy, to be filled
> with light, and to shine."
>
> *(from the poem,*
> *When I Am Among the Trees, 2006, p. 4)*

The winters are long in New England so when we finally get a warm spring day, it has a magical feeling. That's why I wasn't too surprised when, on our first warm April day, Judy said to me, "Can we have our session outside?"

I had never been asked this question by a client before. It reminded me of the times in college when students would vie for class on the lawn. We would assemble picnic-style on the grass and pretend to listen to the professor.

"Sure," I said, "why not?" And thus we had an impromptu session on my back porch, taking in sunshine and warmth. I experienced a different side of Judy that afternoon. She seemed more enlivened and enthusiastically inquisitive about her inner world. She shared parts of her history that were new to me and even lifted her eyebrows at an *ah-ha* moment. Sitting under the blue sky seemed to lift her spirit.

When I first moved to New Hampshire, a friend of mine advised, "Make sure you get outside year round; find things to do outside in the winter besides shoveling snow." This was sound advice, but not for me. My inclination is to hibernate. I literally have to force myself to exit my den during the coldest months. But I do get out for brief blasts of breathing because if I don't, I get a headache (a vague sort of stuffy ache that makes me feel foggy in the brain). I call it *cotton-head.*

As we wrapped up the only session I've ever had on my porch, my client said, "I think that was our best session." I smiled. Although I'd love to believe it was my skill, I suspect it was simply the fresh air working its healing magic on both of us.

Reflection: If you don't intentionally clear your head, with what will it remain cluttered?

TAPS

What: Stimulate your nervous system to wake you up.

Tap ten times on five parts of your body. With one hand, starting with your forehead, tap using the tips of your fingers. Next, finger-tap your inner cheekbones close to your nose using both hands at once. Third, tap the underside of your chin with the side of one hand. Fourth, finger-tap both sides of the chest just under the collarbone with two hands. Last, knuckle-tap both your thighs at once. Finish with a deep breath and exhale, letting your arms relax.

When: When you're feeling exhausted and still facing the end of your day.

Why: This micro-self-care practice is a simplified and adapted technique derived from the field of energy psychology, which includes mind-body approaches such as Emotional Freedom Technique (EFT, e.g., Craig, 2011), Qigong (e.g., Dougherty, 2007), and acupressure (Gach and Henning, 2004). Although skeptics abound, many psychotherapists find these more 'Eastern' interventions effective and helpful. Notice for yourself how tapping your body may variously trigger an increase in energy, calm your mind, reduce your negative feelings, and stimulate your senses.

We're not supposed to have favorites, of course, but sometimes there's a client that we really click with . . . someone who we just enjoy being with, really root for. I had one client like this years ago but she came at 7 p.m., always my last in a long day of clients. Sadly, I felt like she got the dregs of me.

Maggie came from a wealthy family and had suffered tremendously from her father's verbal abusive. Recently married, Maggie was young, smart, and funny. She was also dangerously close to having an affair. Her husband was an international pilot and away for long periods of time. She felt lonely and was looking for attention.

What surfaced for Maggie in our work together was her need to be adored and appreciated. She didn't consciously want to have an affair, but Andy from her gym had invited her to lunch. She found herself encouraging his attentions.

I desperately wanted to help Maggie understand her behaviors and think through the consequence of her actions. Yet every time I saw her, I felt like a dishrag. I've never fallen asleep in a session before, but with Maggie, I came close. I felt guilty that she was getting the used up, end-of-the-day version of me.

This guilt was weighing me down one day as I finished with my sixth client and still had Maggie to go. The previous week, I had suggested to Maggie that she tell her husband the truth about everything she was struggling with. I told her that transparency was necessary for her to have an intimate marriage. I knew that Maggie was at a crossroads for herself and deserved an attentive therapist. It felt almost unethical that I would join her tonight with absolutely nothing left to give.

With ten minutes to lift my mood and energy level, I remembered a technique from an energy psychology CEU workshop and started tapping my body. I moved from my head and neck to my chest and legs. Whether it was the vigorous movement, the moving of my chi, or the release of energy blockages, the tapping really woke me up. I felt my body and then my mind becoming more alert—just in time.

We had a very powerful session in which Maggie touched the roots of her intense attachment needs. In the end, Maggie did avert infidelity-at least for the time being. She had skipped lunch with Andy and opened up to her husband. He took her concerns seriously and planned an overnight weekend for just the two of them.

I'm glad that I was alert enough to be fully there for her.

Reflection: How many clients get the used up version of you?

VICTORY LAP

What: Honor and celebrate your clients' successes, especially an ah-ha moment, whether it occurs inside or outside the session.

Depending on how you physically express celebration, take a moment after a particularly successful session with a client to honor it. Give yourself a high five, or raise your fist into the air and say out loud, "Success!" Or, perhaps even run a small victory lap in your office.

When: After a session with an ah-ha moment or during which your client has experienced real progress toward a goal.

Why: Most of our sessions with clients are micro-movements along what sometimes feels like a very long road to healing. Occasionally we experience a session with an individual, couple, or family that feels like a big leap forward. Or we hear from a client how during this past week, things were different, better, and crystallized into positive change. In the midst of all the suffering we witness, it is essential that we notice and celebrate even the smallest of our clients' successes and healing progress. Honoring the simple victories reminds us of our purpose.

Rosa and Don were seeing me for relationship distress. Rosa was jealous and suspicious. She had been betrayed by her first husband when he cheated on her with her best friend. In fact, although she and her ex were each re-partnered, it still made her crazy when she thought about the deceit.

Now with Don, Rosa felt that she was on the verge of ruining everything. She was aware of her emotional baggage but couldn't seem to stop herself. She wanted Don to account for his every move. She checked his emails and text history. She interrogated him at night and still wasn't satisfied about his whereabouts and motives.

Don said to me, "I feel like I'm a suspect in an FBI investigation." He shook his head. "I love Rosa so much but I just cannot live like this. She has nothing to worry about but her paranoia is tearing us apart."

I had explained to them that emotional safety was a key ingredient in a healthy relationship. Rosa needed to do a combination of her own inner work around past trauma and her capacity to trust, and she also needed to do some healing work with her husband. Don needed to learn to tolerate her distress and begin to share his feelings. I believed that together they could heal their relationship.

A recent example of their distress presented itself in this session. Don had some car trouble and had run into a buddy while waiting for the tow truck. Rosa was convinced that he preferred his buddy's company to hers and might have sabotaged his car on purpose. She knew it sounded crazy but she just couldn't shake the fear that Don didn't want to be with her.

Don looked genuinely dumbfounded when he heard her half-formed theory. He looked crestfallen. "Why don't you get how much I love you?"

I asked him to turn towards her, look her in the eyes, touch her, and tell her why he loves her so much. Don uncrossed his legs, turned towards Rosa, reached for her hands and said, "Baby, don't you get it? I love you more than anything. I love your smile and your laugh. I love that you'll hike with me and pitch a tent. You're my dream come true. *Please* . . . I want you to get it." He began to cry at that point, as did Rosa.

In fact, there wasn't a dry eye in the room.

I asked Rosa if she could feel his authenticity. She nodded. "I want to hold this feeling forever," she said.

I was pleased for them that they had successfully created a beautiful moment of emotional intimacy and bonding. I was excited for Don that he had found his voice and felt safe enough to express his true feelings. And I was happy for Rosa as she learned how to imprint that feeling within her, holding it, expanding it, and absorbing it.

After Rosa and Don left my office, I was overflowing with excitement for them. I wanted to celebrate this moment of two fearful individuals finally meeting heart to heart with love, a small but meaningful success in their relationship. I didn't want to let the moment pass without honoring it. I wanted to do a victory lap—and so I did.

Reflection: What success stories for your clients have gotten lost in your push to finish your day?

CLEAN SWEEP

What: Use physical movement to clear the feelings in your office space.

Holding a tissue or feather, walk around your office swiping at the air and gesturing for any heaviness or negativity to move. Use this motion around the area where your client just sat. Make a "swoooosh" sound as you imagine the negativity moving out and away from your office. You can even sweep the space away from your arms and legs as you engage in this cleansing practice.

When: After a particularly negative or difficult client.

Why: For many, ritualistic movements and sounds, real or imagined, are powerful methods for utilizing the mind-body connection to change thought patterns and shift feeling states. I'm reminded of how a school bell triggers students from raucous chatter to focus and attention or the raising of a flag brings the patriot's hand to her chest, a feeling of gratitude and connectedness to her heart. Let yourself symbolically move negative energy away from your space in a way that brings a feeling of renewed purity. Doing so will help you be ready to meet your next client.

It was 1:20 p.m. and Rachel came to my door, predictably ten minutes early for her appointment. This was our tenth session together and honestly, I had no idea why she continued to come. I was certain that I hadn't helped her in the slightest way.

She originally came to see me because of stress in her life.

Her grown son, age thirty-four, had recently moved back home because he was unemployed and needed financial help. Mom had reluctantly allowed him into her home—even though they had a tense history together—but complained bitterly about him.

One session, she complained about how he left dirty dishes on the counter. The next, she complained about how he created a mess in the TV room. She was enthusiastic about creating ground rules with appropriate consequences, but she always had an excuse as to why she couldn't enforce them.

When she wasn't grousing about her son, she had a list of other woes that included but were not limited to her annoying co-worker, inconsiderate ex-husband, rude niece, and ill-behaved dog.

Rachel wasn't interested in any insightful interpretations or cognitive shifts. She shied away from personal responsibility, didn't really want to talk about her past, and was reluctant to share her emotions. I frequently felt ineffective and flooded by her negativity.

One session was so relentlessly negative that I felt like a sponge, absorbing every heavy thought in her head. I felt helpless, paralyzed, defeated. She spent an inordinate amount of the session talking about her back pain and reporting on physical tests, a cortisol shot, and medical conjectures. I especially do not enjoy hearing a client discuss, in excruciating detail, their medical conditions. By the time she left, I was almost comatose in my seat.

As I closed the door behind her with only a few minutes

before my next client, I wondered how I could shake off this lead-blanket feeling. That's when I took a tissue and began wildly waving my arms through my office—anything to move the stagnant energy and symbolically clear the air. Over time, it has become a post-session ritual that I use when I feel heavy with negativity or hopelessness.

Reflection: Quiet yourself and see if you can feel the subtle differences within after you sweep out challenging energy.

JUMP FOR JOY

What: Energize yourself before a client.

Do two sets of five jumping jacks, stopping between each set to reach for your toes. Begin slowly as your muscles will be tight. Notice how your hands may come closer together with each jump. As your muscles stretch you may be able to clap your hands at the top of the jump. In bending at the waist for the stretch, let yourself hang like a rag doll with your knees slightly bent. Feel the muscles in your lower back and the back of your legs lengthen as you breathe in to the stretch. This practice gets your blood moving.

When: When you are feeling drained and exhausted and you just don't know how you're going to rise to the occasion of another client.

Why: Vigorous exercise simply wakes up your body and pumps oxygenated blood to your brain. The quick pace of jumping jacks elevates your heart rate and wakes you up by increasing oxygen flow to your brain and tired muscles. Hanging down from your waist not only moves blood to your brain but also stretches your hamstrings, which releases tension on your lower back. If you have low blood pressure or other cardiovascular conditions, check with your doctor before doing these exercises.

I was so excited to finally have four days to delve into the intricacies of EFT, Emotionally Focused Therapy, for couples. I had been a fan of Sue Johnson's work (the founder of EFT) for years. I had seen her in person and on tapes as I acquainted myself with her highly effective intervention for couple distress. At the time, I was also knee-deep in researching my book, *75 Habits for a Happy Marriage.* The timing for this training was perfect.

The first day was exhilarating as we combed through the training manual and I imagined using this new method with my clients.

The second day we watched training tapes and a live consultation with a couple. Although the material was riveting, I was starting to feel the effects of sitting for eight hours a day in a windowless conference room.

The third day, although I still found the training quite exciting, in theory, dragged as I struggle to stay awake and keep focused.

By the fourth day, I was wishing that the whole thing was over. I did want to learn about attachment styles, de-escalation phases, and "softening the blamer" protocols, but my energy lagged and my mind was numb from such concentrated attention. It is amazing how quickly we can succumb to the tiring effects of sitting for long periods of time.

Breaking up into small groups to do couple role-play, I greeted my fellow group members with a stifled yawn. Sophie, the youngest among us looked at me and chimed in, "Right? It's hard to sit still for four days. But I have a trick that can help us, if you're game: jumping jacks."

Janice, the most senior among us, chortled skeptically, "I haven't done jumping jacks since I was a girl."

Sophie explained, "I was once in a workshop and the leader actually had the entire audience doing jumping jacks right after lunch. It really woke us up. I've been doing them ever since—better than a cup of coffee." And so together we broke into a series of jumps. Although we got some strange looks from our colleagues, I had to admit that it really got my blood pumping. I felt more awake than on day one.

Even Janice was sold.

Reflection: What differences in energy and alertness do you notice when you move your body?

MIRROR, MIRROR

What: Bring fresh energy to your role as a change agent.

Look at yourself in the mirror, wink, and say out loud (or silently) as you make eye contact with yourself, "You are making a difference in people's lives. You are doing meaningful work." Pick a mirror at home or at work that you identify as your magic mirror.

When: At least once a day.

Why: Most of us who enter the field of psychotherapy are energized by the possibility of emotional change and growth. Still, in the face of the continuous stream of human suffering and trauma that we face, paired with the clients who are resistant to change, we can lose sight of the positive effect that we have on clients' lives. We can feel discouraged.

This self-care practice brings energy to your purpose. It gets to the heart of what self-care is all about: being gentle and kind to yourself. With these simple statements paired with eye contact, remind yourself that your work matters. What you do makes a difference.

I don't think I have a reputation for helping people leave their loveless marriages but I have worked with quite a few clients who have come to me married and left divorced. I don't see it as my job to help destroy or save marriages but rather to help my clients find their own truth.

Ruth was such a woman. She came into my office complaining of insomnia and anxiety. After a few sessions, I discovered that she was deeply unhappy in her marriage. When I suggested she might want to start couples counseling with her husband, she resisted. She told me she didn't see the point. She didn't love him and was tired of living a lie.

Our work together evolved from me listening and supporting to coaching and finally, to cheerleading her initial steps towards a new life. She stopped seeing me after filing for divorce because her finances needed to go towards her legal fees.

Six years later, Ruth returned for a session. She was relocating with her new husband and wanted to have a few sessions regarding her anxiety about starting over. When Ruth walked into my office, I couldn't believe the change. She looked wonderful. She had a glow about her, a twinkle in her eye. She told me that she had never been happier. "I've never forgotten what you said all those years ago. It made all the difference."

I almost never actually remember having said the powerful words that clients attribute to me, but can't help but be impressed if they turn out to have been wise and instructive. Ruth said, "You told me that I *deserved* to be happy. You said that it was my birthright. I always remembered that. I wouldn't be where I am now if I hadn't had your help."

That's what we do. We make a positive difference in people's lives in ways we may never know. Not every client's life, but many of them. In so many ways, we are agents for change. We need to remember that, everyday.

Reflection: Who has made a difference in your life?

GIVE THANKS

What: Bring professional gratitude into your life.

Tell a colleague "Thank you," either in person, by email, phone, text, or letter. Let the feeling of gratitude bring a smile to your face.

When: Whenever you find yourself feeling disconnected from your colleagues or discouraged in your workplace.

Why: When you give thanks for someone, you increase your awareness of gratitude in your life, build feelings of connection, and enhance your social bonds. When you saturate your life with gratitude, you increase your own level of happiness. Being appreciative has been shown to be significantly related to positive life satisfaction and positive emotions (Adler and Fagley, 2005). In spreading good will to your colleagues, you generate a positive affect all around. It's a win-win situation.

I was absolutely exhausted. It was Friday at last, a day that I sometimes take off as a kind of personal fun day. But this Friday wasn't going to be all that fun. It was a perfect seventy-degree, bright and clear New England day but I had plans to attend a six-hour CEU workshop on infidelity. I just wasn't in the mood to sit all day in a windowless hotel conference room. In fact, if I hadn't prepaid for the event, I would have bailed.

I arrived a few minutes late—my own not-so-unconscious resistance. The muffin and bagel tray had already been picked over, the only seats available were on the back row, and the speaker was already speaking. To my surprise, Janis Abrahms

Spring, author of several books including *After the Affair*, was charming. Not only that, but I saw several therapists in the room whom I hadn't seen in awhile. We exchanged smiles and waves as we listened to Janis's instructive stories.

During the break, my colleague Nancy got the gratitude ball rolling. She came over to me at the coffee station and said, "I'm so happy to see you. I wanted to thank you for telling me about that restorative yoga class. I recommended it to my client and it made a huge difference."

Then I saw another colleague who thanked me for a recent referral. Then another from my former consultation group who told me how much she missed my contributions. By the end of the day, I was feeling warm and fuzzy. That night, knowing how difficult it is to lead full day workshops, I spontaneously sent off an email to the speaker, Janis. I told her how much I had appreciated her candor, personal stories, instructive model, and teaching style. She responded with her own gratitude for my email and how much she appreciated my words.

Whether I'm on the speaker side of that podium or in the audience, I know that I absolutely cherish words of gratitude. But even more, I notice that I'm personally enriched when I give expression to it, when I notice that I'm thankful for something and share it with the person who brought that something into my life. Express it, receive it, feel it. Gratitude has a way of expanding when you give it some energy.

Reflection: Do you notice gratitude growing within you as you give thanks?

CHAPTER 7

PRACTICES FOR RELAXING

She sat in front of me fidgeting with her hands. She muttered, "I'm just so stressed. It feels like I never get any time alone. Two kids, two step kids, and a husband means that I never have a second to myself when I get home. They even bother me when I'm in the bathroom. I can't get a minute to myself to relax."

Almost one hour to the minute later, another woman sat in front of me fidgeting with her hands. She muttered, "I'm just so stressed. I feel so lonely. Living alone and not having any pets means I'm completely isolated when I get home. I have to turn on the television just to hear some human voices. I get so anxious being alone that I can't relax."

Let's face it—it can be hard to relax. And obviously, different people relax in different ways. Introverts tend to relax, or replenish, with solitude. Extroverts tend to relax, or replenish, with social interaction.

My favorite macro-self-care practice to rebalance, I must admit, is going on silent retreat. I started going on retreat as an exhausted young mother when my children were little. My fellow mothers were horrified that I would take such extreme measures for self-care. I didn't take the shame bait and kept going on annual and bi-annual retreats. Now, my children and I are no longer young, but those retreats have held steady.

However, if I only relaxed when I was on retreat—once or twice a year—I would be in big trouble. I take my micro-self-care regimen seriously and endeavor to find small ways to relax every day: micro-relaxation.

We know we should relax and certainly want to every day, but when we finally do get some down time, relaxation eludes us. Our minds race in the silence and our thoughts hound us. We search for something to do. We turn to mindless entertainment or to a cocktail to help induce a feeling of respite.

The trouble is that these so-called relaxation techniques don't actually recharge us. They merely distract us or numb our feelings. Just like our clients, we avoid our feelings and look to quick but short lived soothing techniques. Endless amounts of television, video games, web surfing, alcohol, and recreational drug use provide a feeling of temporary relief but at a cost. Our thoughts still run wild and our sympathetic nervous systems (SNS) are still energized. Distraction is not the same thing as deep relaxation.

True relaxation is when the parasympathetic nervous system (PSN) is activated. Whereas we can think of the SNS as the accelerator of our minds and bodies, we can think of the PSN as the breaks. But the PSN doesn't just break our stress response—it also directs our bodies to restore, replenish, and recharge. True relaxation, like the restoration of sleep, takes the dead battery and recharges it.

The micro-self-care practices included in this chapter give you a choice of ways to weave in powerful moments of replenishment and PSN activation into your day, every day.

It's time to unwind and let go, at the office and at home.

UNPLUGGED

What: Go on a digital detox.

Turn the ringer off on your phone, put your computer to sleep, and remove yourself from all screens. Select a period of time (one hour, two hours, half a day) and do not, under any circumstances, use or access your electronic devices.

When: Every day, for a set period of time.

Why: We are living in perhaps the most overly stimulating era in human history. We are forever reachable, accessible, and plugged in. You see people communicating via their phones in subways, on beaches, on safaris, and while hiking remote mountains. Our brains experience some pleasure when we plug in (a data hit). However, for us to retain the awareness and sense of calm that we and our clients deserve, we need breaks from the relentless digital stimuli. Intentional data detoxing allows our own systems a chance to reboot. Think about it—you don't access email during a client session, right? This practice asks you to push beyond that. Give yourself a real break from the constant on-call nature of electronics.

Not too long ago, my colleague, Bill O'Hanlon, and I hosted a "Happiness Habits" Telesummit. We spent a very enjoyable hour interviewing one of the grand dames of the self-help industry, Joan Borysenko. Joan, author of numerous books including, *Fried: Why You Burn Out and How to Revive*, is a pioneer in mind-body medicine. When we asked her about one of her most cherished ways of taking care of herself, she responded without hesitation, "I unplug from my electronics two days every week."

TWO DAYS! I was amazed. I admit that even though I know this would be good for me, sometimes I am hard pressed to go two hours without checking my email. I remember when I got my first smart phone. I was stunned that I could receive emails while out and about. Now, I am sometimes guilty of checking my phone for emails in restaurant bathrooms. It's not that I'm expecting something particularly interesting or important. I have developed the compulsive habit of checking my smart phone, as if awaiting news I've been awarded the Nobel Prize.

What a treat it is to be completely unplugged. Once you get past the initial addictive impulse, your focus shifts. Instead, you can check in on yourself and check up on the world directly around you.

The challenge on our path to self-care is not to make our lives harder by eliminating our tools for communication, nor is it to set unreasonable data silence goals. Our goal is to take the seed of Joan's sound advice, plant it gently, and watch it grow every day.

Reflection: What are you afraid of missing when your phone and computer are shut off?

THERE'S NO PLACE LIKE HOME

What: Transition to your home with gratitude.

Think of three things that you're grateful for about your home. Focus on three aspects or feelings that you're particularly excited to see or experience upon your return.

When: On your commute home.

Why: Gratitude is your fastest shortcut to happiness and inner peace. It's amazing how this simple practice, a gentle refocusing of your attention, can change your mood and attitude. Rick Hanson describes the practice of gratitude as one of the simple ways to change your brain through experience-dependent neuroplasticity. "Soak up the gifts coming to you," he writes, "whatever they are. Let them become part of you, woven into your body, brain, and being. As you inhale, as you relax, as you open, take in the good that you have been given" (2013, p. 81). This micro-self-care practice helps you begin to transition your energy and focus from work to home. Nurturing your appreciation of home and loved ones creates a climate of eager anticipation as well as gratitude. Learn to shift your priorities at the end of the day and arrive home with an open heart.

Stuart lowered his head, defeated. He rested his forehead in his hands and softly began to cry. "I just don't understand," he said. "I cannot imagine moving out."

Stuart and Amy, now in their second session with me, had been married for over twenty-five years. Their life together had always been career- and family-focused. However, now that the kids were off on their own, Amy expected a revival in their marriage. Unfortunately, work seemed to occupy him all the more and she felt like she didn't matter to him at all. Stuart also felt unappreciated. They both wanted something more. Amy was hopeful that a separation would allow her to make some sense of her feelings and whether they could still make their marriage work.

Stuart was shocked. "But I don't want to move out. I love our life together, our home. I love *you*. This isn't what I want."

Amy was insistent. "It has to be this way right now. I have to get my head clear."

By the end of the session, Stuart had agreed to move to a local guesthouse for one month. In that time, they would continue their weekly couples counseling sessions.

During the next month, I witnessed an amazing change. They both became very aware of what they had to lose. Their priorities changed. With his heightened awareness of how much he valued his wife and their home together, Stuart became a very motivated spouse. He began gradually doing the very things that Amy felt had been missing. He complimented her, wanted to spend time with her—basically courted her. His love for her became transparent. Amy, too, was newly appreciative of Stuart's attentiveness and his crucial contributions to their life together.

By the month's end, Amy welcomed him back to their home with open arms. Even six months later, as we ended our work together, they were both surprised at the dramatic shift in their relationship. “I just kind of woke up to what I’d been missing for so many years,” Stuart said. “These last months, each time I drive in the driveway, I am just so grateful for all the things I love about my home: Amy waiting for me, the gardens we planted together, our fantastic back porch, that feeling of connection and familiarity. It feels like a real homecoming.”

Reflection: Notice, do you experience your home differently (do family members receive you differently) when you return home with gratitude on your mind?

THE ULTIMATE REST

What: Relax your body and mind in a classic yogic posture.

Set a timer for up to five or ten minutes then lie down on your back with your arms at your sides and close your eyes. You may use a blanket or foam mat for more comfort. Intentionally relax your eyes, letting them sink back into your head. Let your face and limbs droop toward the floor. Bring your attention to the rise and fall of your chest.

If you prefer a chest opening stretch, a modification is to use a six-inch foam roller or pillows, aligning them under you so that they extend along the length of your spine and under your head. Allow your arms to open wide and your shoulders to drop down, pulled by gravity. Feel how your chest opens with every breath.

When: In the evening before you go to bed or during a break at work.

Why: There are times during the day, especially before bed, when it is crucial to relax our bodies' stress response. In the yogic tradition, the ultimate relaxation pose is called shavasana, a Sanskrit word meaning "corpse pose." If you have been to a yoga class, you have likely finished your session with this classic posture (usually it's a favorite). Research has shown that ten minutes of shavasana acts to decrease blood pressure, heart rate and other indicators of stress. This same research indicates that the body's relaxation response increases with regular practice (Sharma; Mahajan, & Sharma, 2007). Using a support under your spine relieves a fatigued or sore back and counteracts the rounding of your shoulders that you may take on as you become tired.

My license requirements include annual CEU's and collaboration hours. At times I have seen the latter as both a blessing and a curse. Finding the time to squeeze in yet another meeting has sometimes felt like a burden. Still, having been in several different consultation groups over the decades, I can attest to the benefits of joining with others, of many minds, and of the breaking of the isolation of private practice.

For quite a few years, I was in a group that was guided by a paid supervisor. We had live consultations, case presentations, group support, and general camaraderie. One week, our fearless leader asked us to share our favorite self-care strategies. This was particularly interesting to me because in three years we had never discussed the topic. One of our members shared that he went on a spiritual retreat two times a year. I thought this was such an inspired ritual that I myself began to implement regular spiritual retreats.

Another member shared that he had lunch with a dear friend every Friday as a form of social support. I was clearly ripe for self-care because I soon initiated monthly luncheons with my best friend.

But what stands out the most for me from this meeting was the enthusiasm with which one woman shared her discovery of a fabulous new practice for her: restorative yoga, a form of yoga that uses pillows, bolsters, and towels to support the relaxed body in various positions. She would lie every day with her back on pillows and arms draped down, claiming that this practice made her heart feel more open and compassionate toward her clients.

I wish I could say that I immediately adopted this beautiful practice, but I didn't. I forgot about it until years later when my physical therapist recommended a similar posture for back pain. Not only did my back begin to feel better, I really did begin to feel a sense of open-heartedness. You never know when a seed, once planted, will finally bear fruit. Just keep your heart open to possibility.

Reflection: How often do you currently allow your body to open and relax?

TETHER BALL

What: Take a moment to scan your body, heightening your body awareness.

Scan from the top of your head down to the bottom of your feet. Close your eyes and imagine warmth flowing from your head, down your face, your throat, and upper body; feel the weight of it pressing down your arms and hands, over your abdomen, moving heavy over your thighs, knees, calves, and feet. As the warmth moves slowly from one body part to the next, let yourself notice what you are feeling in that area. Do you notice tension, discomfort, blood pulsing, or ease? In the end, observe your body as a whole and notice where you might be holding tension. Just be the observer, inquisitive but not judgmental. Notice changes in feelings and sensations.

When: When you're just not present, your mind is someplace else, or you have lost touch with how you are feeling in your body.

Why: We need to be tethered to our bodies in order to do our best work with full awareness. When your body is no longer in the game, it is a sign that you have lost your dual awareness (simultaneous awareness of your external senses and internal senses), an essential, in-session quality. This dual awareness is basic to our ability to track our clients' emotions as separate from our own. Doing a body scan is a way to rebalance our awareness and stimulate relaxation. In fact, the body scan is a core exercise in Jon Kabat Zinn's successful "Mindfulness Based Stress Reduction" programs (2005). As therapists, awareness of our bodies is essential for monitoring levels of arousal and emotional reactivity during and between sessions.

I have certainly had occasions at work when I felt too excited to be fully present. Usually the cause is bright, sunny weather when I'm aching to be outside. Or it might have to do with some exciting plans for the upcoming weekend.

I've also had a few times when stress in my personal life has challenged my ability to be fully present with my clients. One such time was during my divorce from my first husband. Another was when my second husband, Daniel, was undergoing treatment for colon cancer.

Although both experiences were painful in different ways, I found Daniel's bout with cancer to be especially overwhelming. His treatment was never far from my mind. Frequently, I found myself thinking of some random medical moment even as a client was sharing their deepest struggle. Having a home office made this especially problematic.

Between sessions I would check on Daniel and see if he needed anything, wanted to get up, was hungry or thirsty, or if it was time for his medication. And then, lost in the world of chemotherapy, I would turn around and go back to my office to prepare for the next client. One day during this six-month stint, I was feeling particularly un-tethered, tense, and virtually numb. I slumped in my office chair and decided to check in with my body, one part at a time. *Ahh yes. Connection to me.*

I re-inhabited my body, expanded my awareness, cleared my mind, and relaxed.

In retrospect, I don't even know how I made it through those months. I guess I did what I had to do when I had to do it; we often have no other choice. For me, grounding myself back in my body, checking in with how I was feeling (however that might be), and keeping an awareness of how it changed moment to moment was essential to taking care of myself and, in the end, my clients.

I'm happy to say that Daniel did recover and to date is still in remission. I continue to use this practice as a mainstay of my micro-self-care tool kit.

Reflection: Can you tell the difference when you are firmly rooted in your body and when you are not?

PROGRESSIVE DINNER

What: Reduce body tension and stress with progressive muscle relaxation.

Progressively tense for five seconds and then relax for ten seconds four major muscle groups. As you relax say a cue word or phrase such as "Relax," "I release," or "It's OK," and notice feelings of relaxation enter your muscles. Repeat the cycle of tense and release twice before you move on to the next muscle group. Start with your lower limbs and feet, move to your chest and abdomen, then to your shoulders and arms, and end with your neck and face.

When: After a particularly tense session with an individual, couple, or family.

Why: Progressive muscle relaxation (PMR), now over eighty years old, has been shown to stimulate the body's relaxation response (McCallie, Blum, & Hood, 2006). It has become a standard intervention for stress and pain relief in many clinical settings. This self-care practice, *progressive dinner*, is a modified version of Douglas Bernstein's abbreviated method (2007). For the therapist, its benefits are three-fold: it relaxes the body, focuses the mind, and renews awareness of our feelings and inner sensations. Stahl and Goldstein's *Relaxation and Stress Reduction Workbook*, now in its sixth edition (2008), is an excellent source for a more detailed explanation of the technique.

My first experience with the power of progressive muscle relaxation came after a tumultuous family session. Josie and Leon weren't married but they had lived together for three years. Their problem was that Josie's two adolescent daughters hated—no, despised—Leon. Josie felt torn between loyalty to her teenage daughters and her mate. Leon was tired of the conflict. He felt rejected and had started drinking heavily.

Today, I had all four of them in my office, and I couldn't believe what was happening; Josie had taken a seat next to her two daughters and they were all arguing about Josie's recent decision to include Leon in her will.

I felt like I had completely lost control of the session. Daughter #1 yelled at Leon that he was a drunk loser. "You shouldn't even be in my mother's will at all." Leon rolled his eyes and looked at me, as if saying, "Can you believe what I have to deal with?"

I looked at Josie, thinking she might set some kind of boundary with her daughter, but she merely looked at me helplessly.

Standing up, I motioned to the seat next to Leon and said "Josie, I want you to take this seat next to Leon and talk to your daughters about your decision to include him in your will." She grudgingly moved.

Daughter #2 jumped in, loudly saying, "The money is *our* inheritance. He doesn't deserve a penny of it . . . he's just a gold digger."

Again, Josie was silent, unable to speak her truth. As with

many families whom I've worked with through the years, money is used as an expression of love, a control measure, and a threat.

I looked to Josie and prompted, "Look at your daughters and tell them what you'd like them to know."

With that, Josie burst out heatedly, "I want you to know that I love Leon and that's it's my choice who I put in my will. Besides, there's plenty of money for everyone and I don't plan to die anytime soon."

Shocked at Josie's newfound assertiveness, the room was silent for a moment. Then daughter #2 whispered under her breath, "Plenty of money for freeloaders like *him*."

"Oh, you think *I'm* the freeloader?" Leon responded.

Although the seeds of change had been planted, I could tell the growing season would be long indeed. Their reactivity persisted and by the time they left, I felt as if I had absorbed the tensions of four people—and I had.

I felt like a lead weight was in my stomach. I checked the clock: I had only fifteen minutes until my next session with the sweetest, kindest, most crushed woman I knew. Julianne didn't deserve a tense therapist—she deserved a calm and compassionate presence. She had lost not one but two husbands in the last fifteen years. We'd had only three sessions together, but each time she sat on my couch like a wounded bird, weeping into tissue after tissue.

So, I sat in my chair and turned the tension to relaxation, muscle group by muscle group. With every release, I let the feeling of relaxation fill my body and mind.

By the time Julianne walked up my deck stairs, I had drained myself of the tension from the previous session and was ready to walk the road of grief with her . . . just in time.

Reflection: Where do you carry tension in your body from session to session?

LAVENDER FIELDS

What: Smell your way to relaxation.

Utilize the natural calming effects of lavender scent. Spray lavender mist in your office, smell a lavender sachet, don a lavender eye mask, or use lavender lotion.

When: Between clients or at the end of the day before you go home.

Why: In the world of relaxation techniques, lavender aromatherapy is common practice, whether through soaps, incense, herbal bags, or tea. Today, there is more and more empirical support that the scent of lavender not only reduces stress (e.g., Kim et al., 2011) but also aids in sleep (e.g., Lytle et al., 2014). The scent of lavender's essential oils seems to stimulate a relaxation response in the body. In a relaxed state we, as therapists, are better able to retain the awareness and presence we need to provide good therapy.

We had done the sun salutation, downward dog, cobra, and tree pose. This was a quiet yoga class in a darkened room on a cold winter's day. Ten of us had spent the last hour stretching, pulling, and bending our bodies into pretzel shapes that we were sure would improve our health and well-being.

As the class came to an end, I looked forward to my favorite pose, shavasana (when we lie on our backs, like a corpse, and just rest). I knew that our teacher would come around and gift us each with a short massage and Reiki. But, to my surprise, she added something special this week: she misted lavender water over our heads. The abundance of the aroma settled over me, and with it, a sense of utter calm. I remembered a stroll through lavender fields in French Canada. I conjured images of the ubiquitous lavender bushes I had experienced in Croatia. I was flooded with peaceful memories, a peaceful calm.

I bought myself some lavender water spray after that yoga class and put it in my office with the best of intentions. It wasn't until one day after a particularly emotionally tense session that it called to me again. A couple had come in because they could no longer tolerate each other. Their six-year-old only child had died from an unexpected seizure. It was a heart-breaking loss that had left their relationship in shambles. There was a palpable tension of blame, regret, and shut down emotions in the room. Their deep pain had begun to express itself in anger and resistance to each other.

In the session, I helped them find their pain beneath their resentments. With some guidance, they were able to turn towards rather than away from each other. After they left, I felt pleased with the shift that had just occurred. However, I also felt somewhat dizzy from the dense and heavy energy in the room. My sympathetic nervous system was in hyper-arousal and I couldn't calm myself. I think maybe it was a gift from my unconscious when the answer came to me in a whisper, *lavender.* A few spritzes from the bottle in my closet brought me back to lavender fields and the calming ocean side cafés of Croatia.

Reflection: How do your clients benefit when you are feeling rested, refreshed, and relaxed? What impact do you have on them when you are stressed and fatigued?

SHUT EYE

What: Rest your body with a daytime power nap.

Find a place and position where you can comfortably rest your head and close your eyes. Set a timer to ensure that you do not sleep more than thirty minutes. Depending on your window of time, anywhere from five to twenty-five minutes will be restorative. Feel the tension drain from your body as you rest.

When: When you are experiencing sleepiness.

Why: Although the perfect duration and time for a nap will vary, sleeping for more than thirty minutes will take you into a deep sleep rather than revitalize you. There is a large body of literature showing that the benefits of a short daytime nap range from improved mood and reduced fatigue to improved measures of performance (Milner & Cote, 2009). Adriana Huffington in her book, *Thrive*, leads a crusade against the sleep deprived western world. She writes, "There is practically no element of our lives that's not improved by getting adequate sleep. And there is no element of life that is not diminished by a lack of sleep" (2014, p. 74).

Therapists, especially, are often faced with fatiguing and intensive work environments. A tired body or mind becomes more vulnerable to stress, burnout, compassion fatigue, and secondary traumatization. Thus, sufficient rest is a basic macro-self-care necessity. Naps are the obvious micro-self-care counter-measure to fatigue and poor performance caused by sleepiness. By relaxing into a brief nap, you'll get a subsequent boost of energy and alertness to take you through the rest of your day.

I am a Smith College alumnae and was listening to a video replay of Arianna Huffington's commencement speech to the class of 2013. She said, "You don't get to the top by marrying someone. A much simpler way is to sleep your way to the top."

Did I hear her right? I wondered. *Did she just say what I think she said?* The audience giggled, confused.

"But no," Arianna clarified. "I'm talking about sleep in the literal sense." *Ahhhhh*, I smiled with a sigh as political correctness was restored.

She went on to say that she's something of a sleep evangelist. In 2007, she suffered from burnout, exhaustion, and sleep deprivation to the point where her head fell to her desk, breaking her cheekbone and requiring stitches. Now she speaks relentlessly about the dangers of sleep deprivation in our society. She has even created "nap rooms" at the offices of the Huffington Post.

I'm reminded of my first experience with a power nap as a clinician. I had a small but active private practice at the time, three small children at home, and I worked out of a warm and sunny corner office not far from my house. My youngest was still in diapers and many days I pushed through my clients and professional to-do lists suffering from low to moderate sleep deprivation. This day, in particular, I had been up several times during the night, seen several clients before lunch, and there was just no faking it. How many ways can you disguise a yawn?

Or shift your posture just to keep your eyes open? As I closed the door behind my final morning client, I collapsed on the couch and let my eyes close.

With a jolt, I sat upright in a slight panic. *What time was it? What day was it? Had I missed my next client? Had the sitter called?* It felt like I had slept for hours. One deep breath and a glance at the clock brought me the realization that I had only been out for twenty minutes. Refreshed and with renewed clarity, I ate lunch, finished my case notes, and welcomed my next client. I was blown away by the transformation.

These days, with all three kids off to college, I'm rarely sleep deprived. But I remain a true believer in the effectivenss of the power nap. It is the heaviest hammer in my self-care tool chest.

Reflection: What does it feel like to give yourself permission to rest during the day?

DOODLE BUG

What: Pause from the relentlessness of the day and doodle.

Doodle . . . that's right, doodle. Pick a fresh piece of paper or an old memo and simply watch what happens when you let your pencil or pen move where it will.

When: When you have a client or meeting cancellation.

Why: Artistic endeavors and creative thinking engage the right brain even as they relax the verbal and more goal directed left. There is increasing evidence that doodling, in particular, the random meandering of pencil on paper, engages a brain system that G.D. Schott calls "the wandering mind" (2011). Schott suggests that when we move our attention away from goal-directed activity during doodling, our "attention system" is relaxed. So give your left brain a break, stimulate creative juices and make yourself a more resourceful therapist.

Nancy is my favorite wise woman. At almost eighty years young, she is a fountain of energy and fun. I had never had a friend older than my mother, but age seems irrelevant when you're hanging out with Nancy. I've known Nancy for fifteen years and while I have aged, Nancy seems somehow to have grown younger. Our friendship has spilled out beyond our consultation groups into silly emails and cherished afternoon coffees.

Over time, we've also become CEU buddies. Whenever she's going to a local workshop, she lets me know and vice versa. Nancy likes to get to workshops early and I like to slink in at the last minute. However, Nancy always saves me a seat and so I creep in beside her, quickly making myself look attentive. Nancy, with one ear on the speaker, is always busy doodling in her art journal.

She brings colored pencils and markers for doodling. She brings glittered papers for cutting. She brings her imagination and whimsy. During breaks, I love to look back through her journal. *Oh, there's the ethics seminar from five years ago. There's the couples workshop on infidelity. Oh, I forgot about that anxiety workshop.* Over time I've contributed a few of my own doodle contributions to her journal.

I have never really been a doodler, though, and in fact, find the organic aspect of it a bit intimidating. Still, when my sister-in-law, Christine, introduced me to the art form of Zentangle, I really began to doodle. Zentangle, a copyrighted art form created by Rick Roberts and Maria Thomas, is just systematic enough that it really worked for me. Simple shapes and lines intersect to create complicated patterns. I find it meditative and fun. I like to use the Zentangle template as a springboard for my own designs.

The next time you have a cancellation, avoid the temptation to do paperwork or catch up on emails. Recognize the value of micro-self-care for both you and your clients and relax with some doodling. As your analytic mind relaxes, you'll give your creativity a boost.

The next time I'm in a workshop with Nancy, I'm going to surprise her with my own art journal.

Reflection: Can you let go of the need to be productive every single second?

MUSIC TO MY EARS

What: Reduce your stress response via the magic of music.

Listen to some calming music. Whether you use iTunes, Pandora, CDs, or an old-fashioned record player, stop and listen to a few minutes of music you adore. Don't do anything else—just close your eyes, listen, and allow yourself to be swayed by the music.

When: When you need a relaxing break.

Why: Music speaks to the heart and soul in a way that transcends language. It stimulates soothing images, reminds us of good times, brings people together in community, and moderates our body rhythms. Music, as a therapeutic modality, has been shown an effective intervention to workplace stress (e.g., Smith, 2008). Music is a medium that allows us to intentionally shift away from a verbal world in a way that relaxes our stress response.

"What do you plan to do on your sabbatical?" I asked my friend, Isaac.

For some of my academic friends, a sabbatical means tons of compressed work, research, writing, and publishing. Happily, for this Rabbi, his directive from his large synagogue had been strictly to rest and renew.

"My only plan right now," Isaac replied, "is to listen to music."

"You don't get enough music at synagogue?" I teased.

He mused on this and said, "The thing is, when I'm working, I never really *listen*. I'm thinking about my sermon, or the grieving widow, or the budget meeting. Besides, I want to listen to the Beatles, Jazz, and Spanish guitar music. When's the last time you heard those in a synagogue?"

When indeed? So often we listen to music while we're doing something else: exercising, driving, eating, talking. But listening to music for music's sake can touch us in deep and profound ways. The heightened passion for his favorite music that Isaac expressed is a common experience. I know that for me, music has always felt like a lifeline to my deepest feelings and sense of self.

Another friend had taken her own music therapy to this level. She had recovered from an episode of clinical depression and was now vigilant about self-care. "I'm like a centipede," she said, "I need many, many small legs to keep me moving toward health and away from depression. I can't afford to be lazy about my self-care." Three of her strongest legs were daily exercise, weekly lunch with a friend, and Bach's Brandenburg concerto each and every morning as she showered and dressed.

"In fact," she said, "my daily dose of Bach is my best bet. I just can't feel depressed when I hear Bach in the morning!"

Reflection: What song or type of music really uplifts you?

TRANQUIL SEAS

What: Combine acupressure and deep breathing to induce physical relaxation.

Sitting up with straightened spine (you may find a strait backed chair helpful), find the point on your breastbone, four fingers' width up, from the base of your sternum and press with the fingertips of one hand. Now, breathe slowly and deeply for two to three minutes, paying attention to your breath. Alternatively, you may choose to hold your palms together in a "prayer pose" and depress your breastbone with the knuckles of your thumbs.

When: Between sessions and whenever you want to stimulate a sense of calm and tranquility.

Why: This acupressure point, CV 17, is known to trigger emotional release and relaxation. Michael Gach and Beth Henning (2004) point to CV-17 as the pressure point for relieving anxiety, quelling panic attacks, and calming nervousness. Although acupressure has a millennia long history of emotional healing, only recently has modern science begun to demonstrate the biophysical link between CV 17 and the body's relaxation response (e.g., Yasuzu et al., 2011). *Tranquil Seas* combines acupressure and deep breathing to slow your heart rate and stimulate the parasympathetic nervous system.

It felt like a marathon to me, this, our third consecutive nine-hour day of emotional and intellectual intensity. This was

EMDR (Eye Movement Desensitization Reprocessing) training. I absolutely loved it and was absolutely drained.

Sitting in a hotel conference room with dubious lighting and limited exposure to fresh air is always a challenge for me, even for a standard six-hour continuing education class. But this multi-day, EMDR training required the added drain of emotional intensity, focus on trauma, and the strain of learning and practicing new material. As they say after vigorous exercise, "I was smoked."

But 'smoked' as I was at the end of our final day, I found myself playing 'client' and being asked to relax in the final steps of a body scan. I kept coming up against a tension in my chest. I couldn't relax. The tightness in my chest wouldn't go away no matter how many times my eyes followed her fingers (one of the methods of reprocessing stuck material).

Noticing our struggles, our trainer, Celia, came by to facilitate our learning efforts. "Try putting your hand right here (pointing to the spot on her breast bone)," she said. "Press on it and then breathe deeply." Within a few minutes, the tightness in my chest relaxed. I could breathe more easily. *Wonderful. Amazing. What brand of witchery was this?*

As we were wrapping up, I asked Celia about the technique. "Is it Tibetan, yogic?"

"Actually," she said, "it's an ancient acupressure point," and she referenced the book *Acupressure for Emotional Healing*, by Michael Reed Gach and Beth Ann Henning. This book, which I now own, is an extremely useful manual for self-care and healing.

Reflection: Does self-soothing come naturally to you?

COUNT DOWN

What: Count your way to peace.

Close your eyes and slowly count your exhalations from one to twenty. As you count one, imagine "1" appearing on a big screen. With the second breath, imagine "2" appearing on the screen. With each written number feel yourself going deeper into relaxation. When you notice other thoughts arising, bring your attention gently back to the imaginary screen.

When: Whenever you are off duty but have a client stuck in your head, especially in the evening while transitioning to home or preparing for sleep.

Why: This technique harnesses the mind by focusing your thoughts. The mind can be like a puppy—it goes all over the place until you give it a bone to chew. This particular bone, visualized numbers, allows the mind to refocus and quiet the chatter. The stress cycle between body and mind can feel relentless, with your thoughts triggering stress in your body and your stress triggering thoughts in your mind. This meditative exercise breaks the cycle of repetitive thinking and opens a gap for you to take a new direction.

As therapists, our well-being is proportional to our ability to leave our clients at the office. As we hone our natural skills of empathy and understanding, we also train in maintaining healthy and ethical boundaries. One should not, as I did recently, take their clients on vacation.

Have you ever noticed the irony that just as you're about to leave on vacation to engage in self-care, you're so overwhelmed with the rushed and frantic preparations for departure that you drop your self-care? When this happens, it's easy for your emotional boundaries to weaken.

My husband and I were on an airplane to paradise, but was I present? Was I relaxing? No, I was thinking about my clients. There was the client who had a massive panic attack the day before I left. There was the arguing couple whose relationship was not improving. And there was the widow who told me that she sometimes imagines driving into oncoming traffic to end her life. I had explored her fantasy and ruled out active suicidality. Many grievers wish to die to reunite with their loved one. *Was hers really a normal expression of grief? Was I thorough enough in my suicidality assessment?*

"Excuse me, ma'am," said the flight attendant, "would you like a beverage?"

It seemed that my clients, along with the man I love, were traveling to the beach with me.

That night, even as I was lying on our heavenly bed in our beautiful hotel room, I was still replaying session scenes: the anxious young adult, bitter couple, grieving widow. *ARGH. What was going on?* Usually I had no trouble letting go of clients but, for some reason, they were now stuck in my head.

That's when I closed my eyes and set my attention to *count down* to clear my mind. I followed each exhale like a hawk until my mind drifted down some irrelevant lane . . . *Nope.*

Back to "1" . . ."2" . . ."3" . . . I was ready for sleep before I found my way to twenty.

The rest of the vacation was magical.

Reflection: Are you ever haunted by certain sessions or clients?

TIME TRAVEL

What: Relax by revisiting a pleasant vacation or holiday.

Replace a stressful nighttime routine with a relaxing reverie. Remembering a pleasant time or wonderful vacation, take the time to look through photographs (via photo albums or computer folders). Recall the context and sensory details of each image: where you were, whom you were with, how it sounded, smelled, tasted, and felt. Let the pleasant feelings sink in. Let any sadness of times gone by be eclipsed by gratitude for times you wouldn't have missed. Relax into the wonder of the memory.

When: At night, before bed.

Why: We often hear about the benefits of being in the now. But guess what? Being in the past has a host of benefits as well—the happy past that is. Just as imagined stressful circumstances will prompt your body to respond with stress, so too do imagined and remembered pleasant circumstances prompt your body to relax. This self-care exercise, *time travel*, is based on the same concept as guided imagery techniques, but uses actual pictures to aid in the recollection of a happy time. It is also just plain old good sleep hygiene to replace stressful and stimulating evening activities with those that relax you. So, rather than fill your evening with news, emails, bills, or chores, spend some nostalgic time traveling to the happy past.

I almost always ask grieving clients to bring to session a photograph of their loved ones. I find that it helps me put a face to a name. And for the client, the process of sifting through photos can be therapeutic and cathartic. Only occasionally will a client find that bringing in a photograph is simply too painful.

But not Mimi. When I asked her to bring in a photograph, she actually smiled (the first time, in fact, that I had seen her smile). "I would love to do that," she said. Mimi's beloved husband of thirty-four years had died seven months before. Life without him had left her feeling lost, alone, and rudderless.

When Mimi arrived for her next session, she had a large tote bag filled with albums. She brought her wedding, holiday, and vacation albums. Our session was filled with the recounting of stories as she turned the pages of her life over and over.

She teared up as she shared one precious moment after another. As we neared the end of our time together, she reflected, "It's amazing what a wonderful life we had together."

In our next session, she seemed lighter, almost joyful. She told me that her colleagues were asking if she had started some new drug since she seemed so much happier. She said, "Something shifted for me when we looked at all those photographs last week. I realized that I could fill myself with the sadness of missing George or I could fill myself with the gratitude of all the amazing times that we had together."

As a therapist, is there anything better than observing one of those ah-ha moments, those moments of grace?

Reflection: What pleasant times in your life do you want to revisit?

BALANCED BREATHING

What: Relax your body and stimulate equanimity.

Perform the following steps for alternate nostril breathing. Sit in a quiet, comfortable spot. Place the pointer finger and middle finger of your right hand on your forehead. Place your thumb on one side of your nose and your ring finger on the other. Breathing at a normal and comfortable rate, close your right nostril by pressing your thumb on your right nostril and inhale through your left nostril. Then release your thumb and press your ring finger on your left nostril while exhaling through your right nostril. Next, inhale through your right nostril (while the left nostril is closed off) and then exhale through your left nostril while you close off the right nostril. Always follow an exhale with an inhale using the same nostril. Complete this cycle five times, keeping your attention on the flow of air through your nostrils.

When: When you feel physically attracted to one of your clients.

Why: If you are unhappily single or suffering relationship distress, you are particularly vulnerable to boundary violations with a client. When physical or emotional attraction comes into the foreground of your work with a client, always share your experience with your supervisor or consultation group. Secrecy is your worst enemy.

Still, mild sexual and emotional attraction to a client is natural and common. Micro-self-care is essential for remaining aware and minimizing what might feel like instinctual reactions. Alternate nostril breathing offers the threefold benefit of relaxation, mental focus, and grounding. Following millennia of satisfied yoga practitioners, recent decades have yielded a growing compendium of empirical research demonstrating that alternate nostril breathing slows the heart, lowers blood pressure, and generally stimulates the body's relaxation response (Raghuraj and Telles, 2008). The focus on the breath in this practice mindfully reconnects you with your body and establishes balance. Although there may be gender differences in the body's sexual response to visual and emotional stimulation, there is little debate that the sympathetic nervous system mediates sexual arousal. Thus, self-care practices that prompt the body's relaxation response are crucial for achieving the calm and clarity needed for a healthy therapeutic relationship.

Martha knew she was in trouble when her intake strolled into her room, removed the sunglasses from his eyes, and flashed her a million dollar Hollywood smile. This man was Brad Pitt, Robert Redford, Cary Grant, Antonio Banderas, and Tom Cruise all rolled into one. Martha practically swooned.

The rest of us nodded with understanding. We could imagine such a feeling. We were a tight group of practitioners who had together endured all sorts of professional challenges: audits, cancellations, insurance woes, fee increases, legal proceedings, and compassion fatigue. Being attracted to a client was just one more topic for discussion.

Shelley volunteered, "Did you hear about the psychiatrist

in town who lost his license when he left his wife to run away with a client?" Although this sounded like the set-up for a comedy routine, it was true. While we live with a most obvious ethical standard in our profession (thou shall not have sex with a client), it's understandable that humans in intimate settings find themselves attracted to one another.

Martha was right to share her mild attraction. It opened up a dialogue about the basic human appeal of charismatic people, desire for intimacy, and general sexual attraction. Simply stating and sharing her reaction to this client helped Martha diffuse her feelings of secrecy and taboo. But she was also asking us for specific ways to help her manage her feelings.

Lynn suggested a specific breathing technique. "Whenever I feel out of whack, or off balance, I use the alternate nostril breath to relax myself." She proceeded to demonstrate. I remembered using this during yoga classes.

Martha did balance herself with this practice before the next session with Adonis. With her heightened sense of awareness of her feelings and renewed attention to the professional context of their relationship, she was able to see past his 'perfect' exterior to his wounded inner self. With that, she was in her element.

Reflection: What client characteristics can put you off-balance?

WRING IT OUT

What: Use a spinal twist to relax your muscles and leave your workday behind.

Sit upright in a chair. Slowly and gently twist your body to the right from your hips to your head. Turn around as far to the right as you can, so that you can see behind you. You might wish to grab the chair handle to help you turn further. Hold for ten seconds or longer, allowing your muscles to relax and stretch (as our bodies age, it may take twenty seconds or longer for our muscles to begin to relax and lengthen). Add an extra stretch with a deep inhale, letting your chest expand. Then exhale as you come back to the front. Now, repeat this process to the left, turning as far as you can, holding for ten seconds, ending with a deep inhale, and then exhale upon your return to front.

As you wring yourself from right to left and exhale, imagine you are squeezing out a sponge full of client energy. You may want to repeat each direction more than once to deepen the stretch. Take a moment to notice how your body feels. Once you are done, shake your arms in front of you as you release the day's work.

When: At the end of the workday, before you go home.

Why: The essence of this micro-self-care practice is in the stretch. As we sit in our therapy offices, conference rooms, lunch tables, and in our cars, the muscles of the back, chest, and shoulders tighten and clench to keep our posture. These tight muscles act as reservoirs for our stress and create discomfort and pain. Gentle and slow twisting stretches relax these muscles. Symbolically, this stretch is a way of letting go of the workday. Use it as a ritual to signal to yourself that it's time to leave work at the office and lighten your load for your homecoming.

A therapist colleague in town asked me to come speak to her consultation group on the topic of my new book at the time, *Shortcuts to Inner Peace*. When I met with my colleagues, I shared some of the simple well-being practices that I thought might be useful to therapists. I adapted them, giving them new prompts, such as "Use this one at the beginning of a session. Use this one between sessions." *Aha*. The premise for this book started to come into focus.

I asked my audience, "What is the hardest part of your day?" For many, the end of the day was at the top of the list. Why? Mostly because a therapist has absorbed so much energy by the end of the day that it's both hard to, 1) Leave it at the office, and 2) Have any space to receive the fresh energy of home.

One psychologist said, "I call it the 'full sponge' problem and I think that most of us suffer from it."

I nodded my head and said, "Yes, I know that feeling too. I guess we just need to wring out the sponge." Tapping in to my yoga experience, I led six therapists through a slow and easy cycle of spinal twists. With each twist and exhale, we imagined squeezing out the energy of the day, feeling lighter and more spacious with every stretch.

So, rather spontaneously, right in the midst of my colleagues, this self-care practice was born.

Reflection: What price do you pay at home when you don't find a way to first wring yourself out at the office?

CYCLES

What: Relax the tension in your body as you increase your mental focus.

Perform three to ten minutes of mindful breathing. Breathing normally, keep your attention on the sensation of air against your upper lip or nostrils. Add intention to this basic technique: As you breathe in, think the words, "Breathing in, I am calm." As you breathe out think the words, "Breathing out, I relax." Use a timer to set a comfortable limit.

When: When you have found yourself having a reaction to the emotions, circumstances, or personality of a client. Do this before, during, or after the session.

Why: This relaxation technique, mindful breathing, is so old that it was ancient even to the Buddha himself when he taught it to his followers as a primary spiritual practice 2,600 years ago. It calms the body and the mind. Keeping the mind on the breath focuses our thoughts by anchoring them to the object of our breath. This quiet awareness counteracts hyperarousal and relaxes you in the most basic body function: breathing. Research by Conrad et al. (2006) suggests that paying attention to the breath is the active ingredient in breathing exercises for relaxation. This basic form of mindful breathing is also one of the formal practices in the Mindfulness Based Stress Reduction protocol.

"Kids, we have something important that we need to tell you." The room was still. "Your daddy and I have grown apart (pause) and we feel it's best to get divorced." Silence.

Blink. Blink. I had to mentally pinch myself. I couldn't believe this was happening. I stared blankly at the couple in front of me. They were planning to get divorced and asked me to suggest how they might tell their children. They literally wanted me to spoon-feed them the words, and I obliged. What my clients didn't know is that I myself had used those exact same words seven years previously in my own home, to my own children.

I felt an eerie sense of déjà vu as I imagined my then fourteen-year-old daughter's eyes fill up with tears as she muttered, "No, no, this isn't happening."

The therapy room seemed to spin a bit as I felt some agitation. Right then in the session, unbeknownst to my clients, I launched into a brief *Breathing in, I am calm. Breathing out, I relax.*

Being a couples counselor is rewarding work, but not all couples make it. I've had to counsel quite a few couples on how to break the news of their impending divorce to their children. The children's reactions run the gamut from, "I saw this coming," to crying and screaming and trying to run away. It's never easy. But I had never been asked to specifically role play the part of the parent in the room telling the child, a part I knew only too well.

I got through the rest of the session but the agitation continued. Closing the door after them, I immediately went to my computer to write my case notes as I normally do. But then I stopped. I needed to sit with the enormity of what had been triggered for me. I was experiencing that dreadful sensation of shattering someone's world, of hurting those I loved most.

Breathing in, I am calm. Breathing out, I relax.

Cycles of life. Cycles of families. Cycles of breath.

Reflection: If you don't tend to your own peace of mind, how can you tend to your clients'?

NOW HEAR THIS

What: Let sound calm your nervous system.

For five minutes or longer, make your soundscape be sounds from nature. In an office building, you say? Bring the beauty of modern technology into your day with one of the ubiquitous nature sound apps available on your smart phone. Listen to the sounds of the rainforest, birdsong, wind through the trees, or ocean waves. Listen and focus your attention on the music of nature.

When: When you need a break in the middle of the day.

Why: Listening to sounds around you has a calming and soothing effect. Wallace Nichols, in his book *Blue Mind*, argues that having evolved in natural landscape, humans have an innate attraction to the natural world. Our "blue minds" hold a special affinity for water. Water sounds, in particular, calm our brain and provide a sense of well-being. Empirically, exposure to nature sounds like water and bird song has been shown to speed up recovery from stress (Alvarsson et al., 2010). Turning off the noise in your head and opening your ears to a natural soundscape creates a feeling of inner spaciousness.

Sometimes there's no way around it—a day just flattens you. It could be that you scheduled your maximum number of clients and they all showed up. Or maybe several sessions left you emotionally drained. Or perhaps your home life flooded your every spare moment with something extra to do. Everyone has a tolerance limit. When I stack up busy day after busy day without a respite in sight, I know I'm at risk for a system shutdown.

One was on the horizon, a scheduling overload that could cause me to short circuit. I had seven straight days of intensity: maximum clients, radio shows, writing deadlines, and a two-day CEU workshop. I knew that by the end of this marathon, I was at risk of being in the fetal position, unable to utter intelligible words in my native tongue.

I planned ahead and downloaded a nature sounds app on my phone. One of my strategies was to take time in the middle of each day to listen to five minutes of natural water sounds. *Ah yes*! One day I chose "Australian Beach," the next afternoon, "Tropical Rain," the next, "New England Lake." For my final workday, I chose my personal favorite, "Pirate Ship," (featuring wooden creaking sounds and seagull calls amidst the slap of ocean water).

I grew up in landlocked Dallas, TX. I went to college in western Massachusetts, and I spent eleven years in New York City—an island, to be sure, but I wasn't exactly spending the summer at the Hamptons. When I moved to the seacoast of southern New Hampshire, an entirely new water soundscape opened up to me.

Suddenly I found myself living two miles from the Atlantic Ocean. While it isn't exactly warm enough to swim in (for me), I found myself falling in love with the sounds of the coast. I'd sit and listen to the waves lap onto the beach, the gulls overhead, and even the distant playful chatter of children in the water. In fact, I soon began to choose my vacation spots based on their proximity to the ocean. Something within me had awakened.

Nichols would say I had discovered my "blue mind." Perhaps it hearkens back to my prehistoric ancestors since proximity to water was their lifeblood. Whatever the cause, I certainly love the sound of water.

So how did I do at the end of my busy workweek? I was tired for sure. But thanks to my water app every afternoon, I wasn't in the fetal position after all and I was still able to speak English.

Reflection: What is your favorite water sound?

TRANSPORTATION

What: Use beautiful images to relax.

Look at visually rich, stunning images, either in a book, or on the internet. Take the time to look deeply at the image, noting the tiny details and wider composition. If you are looking at digital images, it is best to create a file of favorites rather than risk the temptation to surf the internet. Still, use caution. This is a case of "know thyself." If digital screens are a source of stress or tend to draw you in to work or random surfing, restrict yourself to hardcopy coffee-table books for this self-care practice.

When: In the small breaks between sessions.

Why: Directing focused attention to a beautiful image directs our brain activity away from chronic thinking and calms our nervous system with positive stimuli. Images have the power to stimulate our imagination, generate real feelings and moods, and thus transport us to another place and time. Trying to fit in one more email, phone call, or session note has an over-stimulating effect on your nervous system, while resting with a beautiful image calms and restores.

It was my last day at my first internship. It had been a wonderful experience working with families, couples, and individuals. I had learned so much from my supervisor, Vince, as well as from my fellow interns. I felt tearful as I went into my last supervisory meeting. I was twenty-six years old.

Vince said, "I know that you're going to be a wonderful

therapist. You've got the heart and you're developing the skill." Then, he handed me a small wrapped package. I was too moved for words.

I opened the gift and found a miniature art book, a collection of Georgia O'Keeffe color plates called *One Hundred Flowers*. It was beautiful. I still have it in my office.

Vince said, "It's small enough to keep in your desk drawer. So this is my advice. Look at the pictures between sessions. Use these images to remind yourself of beauty. You'll be tempted to use every minute between sessions to return phone calls and write session notes. Look at this instead." (Little did he know, in 1988, how many more distractions would become possible with the dawn of the internet).

Vince didn't use the term *micro-self-care*, but that's exactly what he was teaching me. I leafed through this exquisite little book and thought of my art history teacher in college. She told her students, "Look into the painting. Let the technique, composition, and historical context drop away. Gaze deep into the painting and let it touch you. Let it move you. Let it transport you to another place and time."

Yes, let it transport me.

As my career progressed, I assembled a small collection of coffee table books, books with gorgeous glossy images. I have a few go-to favorites that include books on polar bears, beaches and sea glass, cathedrals, rose gardens, and puppies. Through the years, in the spaces between clients, I have sometimes had to force myself away from just-one-more-task to rest my eyes on these pages, letting the images sooth lighten, and transport me.

And then, technology intervened, this time in my favor. Although I still prefer the old-fashioned experience of flipping a page, through digital imagery I can be instantly transported to amazing art and nature visuals I had never imagined: animals and landscapes from around the world, every flower imaginable, collections of my favorite things. Transportation is vast and instantaneous.

Recently, a colleague sent a link to a stunning natural landscape. She gets one in her inbox every morning. She told me that she cannot start her day without first clicking on this email. I told her I understood.

Reflection: What images stir your soul most deeply?

TENNIS, ANYONE?

What: Roll out your muscle tension with self-massage.

Keep a tennis ball in your office closet or desk drawer. Begin in your chair and place the tennis ball under one thigh. Let your weight do the work as you move the ball around your muscles. There may be some discomfort as the muscle fibers loosen and stretch. When you find a trigger point or knot in your muscle, hold the ball steady for about twenty seconds while the tension releases. Next, do the same as you roll the ball down the back of your leg, massaging your hamstring muscle, pausing at each trigger point (you'll know them because they hurt!). Switch to the other leg.

Now remove your shoes and stand on the ball of one foot at a time. Allow as much pressure as you can handle, rolling the ball around the bottom and sides of your foot, pausing for extra pressure at each trigger point. You can also stand against a wall, using the tennis ball to reach areas of your back. Reach and roll it.

When: When you notice muscle stiffness, tension, or discomfort after too much sitting or a tense session with a client.

Why: Trigger point release or active release techniques are self-massage practices that target specific muscles and myofascia (a thin connective tissue that wraps your muscles). The pinpoint pressure of a hard ball allows one to focus pressure at the very points where muscle tissue or myofascia have knotted. As therapists, we are prone to muscle tension. Long hours holding the same posture, in a job that requires little physical movement, in an environment rich with suffering and trauma—it's no wonder we become stiff. Lauren Bertolacci, fitness expert and author of the book, *Tennis Ball Self Massage*, could be speaking to therapists when she writes, "Muscles are on stretch that shouldn't be. Areas are tight that need to be loose, and we are pulling ourselves in all sorts of directions" (2013, p. 2).

It felt like we had been avoiding this moment since our first session.

"I'm going to have to leave," Brad said, choking back tears. "I just don't think I can live this way anymore."

Stephanie replied, "I know . . . I get it. I do."

Brad sobbed openly. "I thought I could make it work. But it's just too *lonely*."

Stephanie said nothing at first, every muscle in her body resisting an emotional response, keeping her safe from whatever she was afraid of. "I wish it was different but it just isn't," she said.

It was heartbreaking to watch this scene unfold. Despite my own awareness, I could feel myself tensing too. Unintentionally mirroring Stephanie's stiff posture, I could feel the chill of her deep seated fear.

Stephanie and Brad had come to see me for marriage counseling. They had two teenagers together and wanted to save their marriage. The problem was that Stephanie didn't want to have sex anymore. It had started slowly, years ago, with their sex life going from every other week, to once a month, to twice a year, to once a year, to not at all.

Over several months together, we had explored this dilemma, their emotional depths, intimacy needs, and attachment styles. But Stephanie stayed aloof, outwardly and inwardly holding back. She wasn't attracted to another man or woman. She didn't watch porn or masturbate. She wished it were otherwise but she just absolutely didn't want a sex life.

Perhaps Stephanie did have some deep emotional work to do, maybe she was holding some long ago trauma, I'll never know. But to Brad she was unwavering: she loved him but she didn't want to have sex.

Brad deeply desired a healthy sex life. He loved Stephanie and their life with their two children. He couldn't imagine splitting up their assets, leaving their home, and sharing custody of their children. His parents had divorced and he wanted to do everything he could to avoid that fate for his own children.

And yet, here he was uttering words that he never wanted to say: "I have to leave."

And here I was, every muscle tense in response to Stephanie's resolute stance in the face of Brad's deep sorrow. I could feel the tension in my feet and legs, my hips and shoulders. My body had recorded the battle between deep sorrow and resistance, between the heat of Brad's love and the chill of Stephanie's distance.

Slowly, after Stephanie and Brad left my office, I began to

erase that emotional recording one muscle at a time, holding that tennis ball at every recalcitrant trigger point. A self-massage had never felt so good.

Reflection: Where do you feel tension in your body when you rise from that final client of the day?

SKY DIVE

What: Relax into the wonder of the sky.

Go outside or to your window and look high up to the sky. Can you see an image in the clouds? What color is the sky today? Know that the spaciousness above mirrors the spaciousness within you. For a different experience, imagine gravity has let you go and you are able to move into the colors of the sky and texture of the clouds. Imagine what it would be like to float on the breeze and look below, as if you had the viewpoint of a bird. Feel yourself expand into the wide, wide world.

When: After a session in which you felt powerless, helpless, or ineffective.

Why: Much of the tension in our lives is the result of supporting our own ego—protecting, hiding, glorifying, fixing, comparing, and empowering our vulnerable and separate self. Yet, in our braver moments, when we are able to open our hearts and expand our perspectives, we let our guard down and relax. Having a lousy session and feeling ineffective is one of those situations that can cause us to lose perspective and feel unsure. The result is tension and stress. Looking up at the sky is a prompt to get out of our own heads, and remember our connection to something larger than ourselves.

It's not easy to be new to this field. I still remember some of my bigger, what seemed to me epic, failed sessions. One, in particular, stands out in my mind. A mother and her twenty-seven-year-old daughter had come to see me for grief counseling. The very wealthy father had died six months previously and left a sizable fortune to his wife.

As we began the intake session, I started asking about the father and how he had died. The mother interjected, "Actually, what's more pressing is the fact that Courtney is dating a boy I don't approve of."

Courtney rolled her eyes. "I don't really care what you think, mother. I am in love with Taylor and you can't stop me from dating him."

"Actually I can," she said coldly. "If you keep seeing him, I will cut you out of the will."

I felt like I was watching a television drama. Courtney practically leaped out of her chair. "Go ahead," she said, the volume of her voice rising, "I'll call your bluff. Just don't expect to ever see any grandchildren!"

Karen, the mother, looked at me and said steadily, "Her boyfriend Taylor is completely unsuitable. He's uneducated, rude, and slothful."

Honestly, I didn't know what to say. *Did the mother make an appointment with me so I would side with her? Did she expect me to slap Courtney's wrists and convince her that Taylor was bad news?*

"It can be frustrating that we cannot control who other people fall in love with," I finally said.

Karen looked at me and said, "But I *can* control my money—no money for Courtney, now or ever."

I tried a different tactic, "Karen, tell me about your relationship with Courtney before your husband died."

Karen didn't seem to hear me. "I hate that boy and I want her to end her relationship with him," she stated icily.

I was thrown off course by Karen's single-minded rampage against this poor boy. I tried exploring her grievances about him. I tried exploring if anyone ever tried to control her choices in a partner. I tried eliciting compassion between them. Finally, I repeated that her adult daughter's choices are not within her control, just as her daughter cannot control her mother's choice in a new partner.

This last comment was a mistake. Karen chastised me for being insensitive. She, as a widow, would never choose to partner again.

My words had not landed, had made no impact. I was spitting in the wind and I knew Karen would never return for another session. As they left, Karen said, "Honestly, I don't know why I came here today. This meeting was a waste of my time and my money."

As they left, I felt I had failed them both. I sat for a few minutes feeling helpless and wondering what I could have done differently. *I had missed my opportunity to develop a therapeutic alliance. What might a more experienced therapist have said or done? How could I have made some kind of positive impact?*

Still berating myself, I went to the window and looked up at the sky. *Sky diving.* I soared in my mind's eye from earth to sky. I gazed at the clouds. I imagined that robin's egg blue sky wrapping around the entire planet. I imagined flying up, being part of that infinite spaciousness.

Suddenly, my shoulders relaxed. My failed session didn't feel so big after all.

Reflection: How do you feel when you realize you are only a small part of a much larger world?

BY CANDLELIGHT

What: Turn writing into an exercise in relaxation.

Light a candle directly in front of you. Gaze into the depths of the flame. Focus your attention on the wisps of flame as they dart out from the wick. Leave the candle burning as you catch up on paperwork. When you blow out the flame, watch the smoke curl and dissipate until that very last moment when all is still.

When: While you write session notes, an article, meeting notes, and emails.

Why: Candlelight is mesmerizing. We intuitively respond to it. In a world of electricity and fluorescent lighting, candlelight both stands out and draws us in. It creates a mood of calm, creativity, and sacredness. It has a slow and still quality that brings us to our center. It quiets and relaxes our minds even as it transports us to a simpler time. Let the candle flame cast its hypnotic spell.

My first husband, David, wanted desperately to live in an antique home. When we chose to move to New Hampshire from New York City, finding a historic home was a top priority for him. Coming from Manhattan with small children, having a backyard was my top priority.

We searched from town to town looking at colonials and antique farm houses, but nothing was quite right . . . until we found the one: an elegant farm house two miles from the coast. David swooned over wide-board pine floors and original hardware on doors and cupboards. I swooned over the acreage. Neither of us was bothered by the sloping floors, curious historic details, or low slanting ceilings.

And so it happened that we developed a fondness for the historic aspects of eighteenth century living. We made our own apple cider, cooked in the fireplace, and every once in awhile, lit the house by candlelight. I was soon to learn, however, that candlelight by choice is quite different than candlelight by necessity.

I have always been a stickler for meeting deadlines. In school I was one of those neurotic, OCD types who never had to pull an all-nighter because I turned in my assignments a day early. I was ill prepared when I found myself without electricity after a winter storm with a deadline for presentation handouts due the very next morning.

It was a bitterly cold, snowy, late January night. I was just sitting down at my computer and the lights flickered, came back on, flickered again, and then all was dark. I couldn't believe it. *How could this be happening?* Panic began to arise in my chest.

But wait, I thought to myself. *Folks have been living in this house for over two hundred years, most of that time without electricity. They had managed by candlelight.* Thinking of the hundreds and thousands of writers who through the centuries had written by candlelight, even been inspired by candlelight, I placed several tall candles around my desk, pulled out a pad of paper, and wrote longhand. At times, I found myself so mesmerized by the flames, their low blue light and dancing flashes of illumination, that I was hard pressed to keep writing.

Fortunately, the electricity was back on by morning. I typed up my notes and had my handouts ready. Just in time.

Reflection: What emotion does a simple flame evoke within you?

LIFELONG SELF-CARE

For centuries, monastic traditions have created and lived by "Rules." Perhaps the most famous is the sixth century Rule of St. Benedict (which is approximately one hundred pages, depending on the translation). A monastic rule is more mission statement than commandment, and is all about guiding individuals down the path they've set out for themselves. In other words, having a Rule is about intentional living.

Once, while on spiritual retreat, I was given the very interesting invitation to create my own personal rule of life. I was advised to think of it as a compass for optimal living. "Keep it simple and start with your relationship with yourself," the Brother said. "That's really the foundation, isn't it? Once you've got that down, you can focus on your relationship with others and your relationship with spirit."

He reminded me that self-love (and the care for that self) is the core prerequisite for all other relationships. As I reflected on this, I decided to make self-care part of my personal rule. Micro-self-care is the daily path, a path that leads to clarity and possibility in one's relationship with others.

We all live by some set of rules, whether implicit or explicit. Have you ever thought about the rules you live by? Are you living with intention? Are you living in a way that honors and nurtures your inner world and your mission as a helper? Your rules and your life path are unique. My hope is that the practices in this book will relax, restore and energize you along that path.

It's never too late to care for yourself. It's never too late to honor yourself as a precious instrument for therapeutic work. Start today and then start again every day, knowing that self-care is the basis for inner peace, compassion, and generosity. Enjoy the lifelong journey as it changes and evolves over time. Remember, when your cup runneth over, you have an abundance to share with the world.

May you be moved by passion and enthusiasm for your work.
May you deeply believe that you deserve self-care.
May you replenish yourself daily.
May inspiration be a guiding compass to your days.
May you know you are a bright light in a world that needs your presence.
May you be an instrument of help and healing.
And may your cup overflow so that there is plenty to share.

REFERENCES

Adler, M. G. and Fagley, N. S. 2005. Appreciation: Individual differences in finding value and meaning as a unique predictor of subjective well-being. *Journal of Personality*. 73(1), 79–114.

Alvarsson, J. J., Wiens, S., and Nilsson, M. E. 2010. Stress recovery during exposure to nature sound and environmental noise. *International Journal of Environmental Research and Public Health*, 7, 1036–1046.

Baraz, J. and Alexander, S. 2010. *Awakening joy: 10 steps that will put you on the road to real happiness.* New York: Bantam Books.

Bernstein, D., Carlson, C. R., and Schmidt, J. E. 2007. *Progressive relaxation: Abbreviated methods.* In: Lehrer P and Woolfolk R (eds) Principles and practice of stress management. New York: Guilford Press, . pp.88–122.

Bertolacci, L. 2013. *Tennis ball self massage: Stop your muscle and joint pain.* Laurensfitness.com.

Bodhipaksa. 2010. *Living as a river: Finding fearlessness in the face of shange.* Louisville, CO: Sounds True, Inc.

Boroson, M. 2009. *One-moment meditation: Stillness for people on the go.* New York: Winter Road Publishing.

Borysenko, Joan. 2012. *Fried: Why you burn out and how to revive.* CA: Hay House.

Bush, A.D. 2007. *Transcending loss: Understanding the lifelong impact of grief and how to make it meaningful.* New York: Berkley Books.

Bush, A.D. 2011. *Shortcuts to inner peace: 70 simple paths to everyday serenity.* New York: Berkley Books.

Bush, A.D. and Bush, D.A. 2013. *75 habits for a happy marriage: Marriage advice to recharge and reconnect every day.* Avon, MA: Adams Media.

Chadwick, Alaya. 2010. *Wake up to your (w)hole life: Discover your hidden strategies and reveal your (w)holeness*. iUniverse.
Chodron. P. 2000. *When things fall apart: Heart advice for difficult times*. Boston, MA: Shambhala.
Chodron. P. 2007. *Don't bite the hook: Finding freedom from anger, resentment, and other destructive emotions* (audio). Boston, MA: Shambhala Audio.
Conrad, A., Müller, A., Doberenz, S., Sunyoung, K., Meuret, A. E., Wollburg, E. and Roth, W. T. 2007. Psychophysiological effects of breathing instructions for stress management. *Applied Psychophysiological Biofeedback*. 32:89–98.
Covey, S. 2004. *The 7 habits of highly effective people: Powerful lessons in personal change, Rev. ed.* Detroit, MI: Free Press.
Cousins, N. 1983. *Anatomy of an illness*. New York: Bantam Doubleday Dell.
Cozolino, L. 2004. *The making of a therapist: A practical guide for the inner journey*. New York: Norton.
Craig, G. 2011. *The EFT manual, 2nd ed.* Fulton, CA: Energy Psychology Press.
Dougherty, Patrick. 2007. *Qigong in psychotherapy: You can do so much by doing so little*. Spring Forest Publishing.
Eden, D. 2008. *Energy medicine*. New York: Jeremy P. Tarcher.
Frankel, D. 2012. *Hope springs*. Columbia Pictures, Metro-Goldwyn-Mayer.
Frankl, V. 1959. *Man's search for meaning*. Boston, MA: Beacon Press.
Gach, M. R. and Henning, B. A. 2004. *Acupressure for emotional healing*. New York: Bantam Dell.
Garcia, R. 2008. *In treatment*. HBO.
Halifax, J. 2009. *Being with Dying: Cultivating Compassion and Fearlessness in the Presence of Death*. Boston, MA: Shambhala.
Hanh, T. N. 1999. *The miracle of mindfulness*. Boston, MA: Beacon Press.
Hanh. T. N. 2011. *The long road turns to joy: A guide to walking meditation*. Berkeley, CA: Parallax Press
Hanson, Rick. 2013. *Hardwiring happiness: The new brain science of contentment, calm, and confidence*. New York: Harmony.
Hanson, R. and R. Mendius. 2009. *Buddha's brain: The practical neu-*

roscience of happiness, love & wisdom. Oakland, CA: New Harbinger Publications, Inc.

Hess, U. and Blairy, S. 2001. Facial mimicry and emotional contagion to dynamic emotional facial expressions and their influence on decoding accuracy. *International Journal of Pschophysiology*, 40, 129–141.

Horneffer-Ginter, K. 2012. *Full cup, thirsty spirit: Nourishing the soul when life's just too much*. CA: Hay House.

Huffington, Arianna. 2014. *Thrive: The third metric to redefining success and creating a life of well-being, wisdom, and wonder.* New York: Harmony.

Jackson, M. 2010. *Temple Grandin*. HBO Films.

Johnson, S. M. 2004. *The Practice of Emotionally Focused Couple Therapy: Creating Connection, Second Edition.* New York: Brunner-Routledge.

Kabat-Zinn, J. 2005. *Wherever you go, there you are: Mindful meditation in everyday living.* New York: Hyperion.

Katie, B. and Mitchell, S. 2003. *Loving what is: Four questions that can change your life.* New York: Three Rivers Press.

Krech, G. 2011. *A Natural Approach to Mental Awareness*. Monkton, VT: ToDo Institute.

Kim, S., Kim, H., Yeo, J., Hong, S., Lee, J., and Jeon, Y. 2011. The effect of lavender oil on stress, bispectral index values, and needle insertion pain in volunteers. *The Journal of Alternative and Complementary Medicine*. 17(9), 823–826.

Kottler, J. 2010. *On becoming a therapist, 4th ed.* San Francisco, CA:Jossey-Bass.

Lytle, J., Mwatha, C., and Davis, K. K. 2014. Effect of lavender aromatherapy on vital signs and perceived quality of sleep in the intermediate care unit: A pilot study. *American Journal of Critical Care*. 23 (1), 24–29.

McCallie, S, M., Blum, M. C., and Hood J, C. 2006. Progressive muscle relaxation. *Journal of Human Behavior in the Social Environment*, 13, (3), pp.51–66.

McGonigal, K. 2009. *Yoga for pain relief: Simple practices to calm your mind and heal your chronic pain*. Oakland, CA.: New Harbinger Publications.

McGonigal, K. 2011. Hugging yourself reduces physical pain.

Retrieved from http://www.psychologytoday.com/blog/the-science-willpower/201105/hugging-yourself-reduces-physical-pain. Psychology Today.

McGonagill, L. 2012. *The light workers healing method: BE who your soul wants you to be*. New York: Morgan James Publishing.

Miller, R. W. & Rollnick, S. 2002. *Motivational interviewing: preparing people for change*, 2nd ed. New York: The Guildford Press.

Milner, C. E. and Cote, K. A. 2009. Benefits of napping in healthy adults: impact of nap length, time of day, age, and experience with napping. *Journal of Sleep Research*. 18: 272–281.

Moss, A. S., Wintering, N., Roggenkamp, H., Khalsa, D. S., Waldman, M. R., Monti, D., and Newberg, A. B. 2012. Effects of an 8-week meditation program on mood and anxiety in patients with memory loss. The *Journal of Alternative and Complementary Medicine*. 18(1), 48–53.

National Institute for the Clinical Application of Behavioral Medicine. 2011. 24th Annual Conference. Hilton Head, NC: Author.

National Sleep Foundation. 2014. ABC's of ZZZZs—when you can't *sleep*. Retrieved from http://sleepfoundation.org/how-sleep-works/abcs-zzzzs-whenyou-cant-sleep. sleepfoundation.org.

National Sleep Foundation. 2009. *National Sleep Foundation 2009 Sleep in America Poll: Highlights & key findings*. Retrieved from http://sleepfoundation.org/sites/default/files/2009%20POLL%20 HIGHLIGHTS.pdf. Sleep foundation.org.

Neff, K. 2011. *Self-compassion: The proven power of being kind to yourself*. New York, William Morrow.

Nichols, W.J. 2014. *Blue mind: The surprising science that shows how being near, in, on, or under water can make you happier, healthier, more connected, and better at what you do*. New York: Little, Brown, & Company.

Norcross, J.C. and Guy, J.D. 2007. *Leaving it at the office: A Guide to psychotherapist self-care*. New York: The Guilford Press.

O'Hanlon, B. and Bertolino, B. 2011. *The Therapist's Notebook on Positive Psychology: Activities, Exercises, and Handouts*. New York, NY: Routledge.

O'Keeffe, G. 1987. *One hundred flowers*. New York, NY: Alfred A. Knopf.

Oliver, M. 2007. *When I Am Among the Trees. Thirst: Poems*. Boston: Beacon Press.

Oz, F. 1991. *What about Bob?* Buena Vista Pictures.

Raghuraj, P, and Telles, S. 2008. Immediate effect of specific nostril manipulating yoga breathing practices on autonomic and respiratory variables. *Applied Psychophysiological Biofeedback*. 33, 65–75.

Ramis, H. 1999. *Analyze this*. Warner Bros.

Ramis, H. 2002. *Analyze that*. Warner Bros.

Ringer, J. 2006. *Unlikely teachers: Finding the hidden gifts in daily conflicts*. Portsmouth, NH: OnePoint Press.

Roach, J. 2004. *Meet the Fockers*. Universal Studios.

Roberts, R. and Thomas, M. 2012. *The Book of Zentangle*. Whitinsville, MA: Zentangle Inc.

Rothschild, B. 2006. *Help for the helper: The psychophysiology of compassion fatigue and vicarious trauma*. New York: Norton.

Schott, G. D. 2011. Doodling and the default network of the brain. The Lancet. 378(9797), 1133–1134.

Seinfeld, J. 2014. Seinfeld-Public-Speaking. Retrieved from https://www.youtube.com/watch?v=yQ6giVKp9ec

Sharma G; Mahajan K. K.; and Sharma L. 2007. Shavasana—a relaxation technique to combat stress. *Journal of Bodywork & Movement Therapies* 11 (2): 173–80.

Siegel, D. J. 2007. *The mindful brain: Reflection and attunement in the cultivation of well-being*. New York: Norton.

Siegel, D. J. 2010. *The mindful therapist: A clinician's guide to mindsight and neural integration*. New York: Norton.

Siegel, R. D. 2009 *The mindfulness solution: Everyday practices for everyday problems*. New York: The Guilford Press.

Smith, M. 2008. The effects of a single music relaxation session on state anxiety levels of adults in a workplace environment. *Australian Journal of Music Therapy*. 19, 45–66.

Spring, J. Abrahms 1997. *After the affair: Healing the pain and rebuilding the trust when a partner has been unfaithful*. New York: William Morrow.

Stahl, B. and E. Goldstein. 2010. *A mindfulness-based stress reduction workbook*. Oakland, CA: New Harbinger Publications, Inc.

Streisand, B. 1991. *The prince of tides*. Columbia Pictures.

Suzuki, S. 1970. *Zen mind, beginner's mind: Informal talks on Zen meditation and practice*. New York: Weatherhill.

Talbott, S. M. 2007. *The cortisol connection: Why stress makes you fat and ruins your health—and what you can do about it*. Nashville, TN: Hunter House.

Talbott, S. M. 2011. *The secret of vigor: How to overcome burnout, restore metabolic balance, and reclaim your natural energy*. Nashville, TN: Hunter House.

The Foundation for Inner Peace. 1985. *A course in miracles*. Tiburon, CA: Author.

Tolle, E. 1999. *The power of now: A guide to spiritual enlightenment*. Novato, CA: New World Library.

Tolle, E. 2003. *Stillness speaks*. Novato, CA: New World Library.

Treadway, D. 2004. *Intimacy, change, and other therapeutic mysteries: stories of clinicians and clients*. New York: Guilford Press.

Van Dernoot Lipsky, L. and Burk, C. 2009. *Trauma stewardship: An everyday guide to caring for self while caring for others*. San Francisco, CA: Barrett-Koehler.

Van Sant, G. 1997. *Good will hunting*. Miramax Films.

Wicks, Robert J. 2008. *The resilient clinician*. England: Oxford University Press.

Yasuzu, K. Munenori, M., Tatsuyo, I., Atsushi, Y., Toshinori, K., Junichiro, H. 2011. Acupuncture to Danzhong but not to Zhongting increases the cardiac vagal component of heart rate variability. *Autonomic Neuroscience: Basic and Clinical*. 162, 116–120.

INDEX